OUR NATION'S DOCUMENTS

Published by Liberty Street,
an imprint of Time Inc. Books, a division of Meredith Corporation
225 Liberty Street
New York, NY 10281

LIBERTY STREET and TIME For Kids are trademarks of Time Inc.

ISBN: 978-1-68330-071-7
Library of Congress Control Number: 2017961429

First edition, 2018
1 QGV 18
10 9 8 7 6 5 4 3 2 1

We welcome your comments and suggestions about Time Inc. Books.
Please write to us at:

Time Inc. Books
Attention: Book Editors
P.O. Box 62310
Tampa, FL 33662-2310
(800) 765-6400

timeincbooks.com

Time Inc. Books products may be purchased for business or promotional
use. For information on bulk purchases, please contact Christi Crowley in
the Special Sales Department at (845) 895-9858.

TIME for KIDS

OUR NATION'S DOCUMENTS

The Written Words that Shaped Our Country

By the editors of TIME FOR KIDS magazine

with Melanie Kletter

Illustrations by Aaron Meshon

★ CONTENTS

INTRODUCTION

You've most likely heard of the Declaration of Independence and the U.S. Constitution. But have you ever actually read them? Many kids—and adults—haven't, and yet these documents are key to understanding our nation. They laid out bold and new ideas that became the foundation of our country.

The Declaration and Constitution were the first documents that would shape our nation. There are others, too, that you'll learn about

Throughout this book, you will be introduced to the people who wrote each document. But many other people affected the policies and words that went into the final documents, from political advisers and public figures to foreign leaders and the everyday Americans who longed for change. You'll meet some of these people in this book, too.

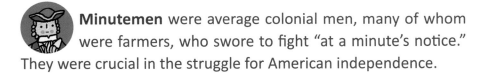 **Minutemen** were average colonial men, many of whom were farmers, who swore to fight "at a minute's notice." They were crucial in the struggle for American independence.

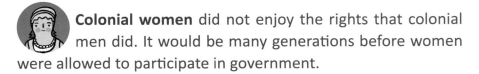 **Colonial women** did not enjoy the rights that colonial men did. It would be many generations before women were allowed to participate in government.

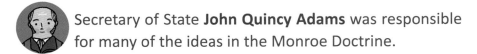 Secretary of State **John Quincy Adams** was responsible for many of the ideas in the Monroe Doctrine.

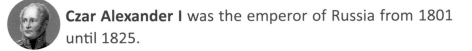 **Czar Alexander I** was the emperor of Russia from 1801 until 1825.

in this book. These documents are presented here in their original form, using the same words and phrases our country's leaders wrote so long ago. But the English language has changed a lot since that time. You will see that many words in these documents are spelled differently from the way they are spelled today. And many words and phrases that were common long ago are no longer used.

While some of the words we use may have changed, the ideas remain the same. Reading historical documents teaches us about our past, and helps us understand our present. By studying these texts, we can find out where our country has been, and where we hope to go.

 Frederick Douglass was born enslaved, but escaped when he was 20. He became a famous writer and speaker.

 Farmers suffered during the Great Depression. Many of the policies of President Franklin Delano Roosevelt's New Deal helped them regain their footing.

American schoolchildren in the 1950s and 1960s were the first to grow up during the Cold War. Every aspect of their lives would be affected by the U.S.-Soviet standoff.

 Joseph Stalin was the leader of the Soviet Union from 1924 to 1953.

Dean Acheson was secretary of state for President Harry S. Truman.

THE DECLARATION OF INDEPENDENCE

Approved July 4, 1776

Thomas Jefferson

The Declaration of Independence is one of our country's most important documents. Its purpose was to announce and explain the reasons why the 13 colonies wanted to separate from Britain. It also included a guiding set of principles for the colonies.

This document was written after the start of the Revolutionary War. The war had begun in 1775. By 1776, colonial leaders had decided it was time to run their own affairs. On June 7, 1776, Virginia delegate Richard Henry Lee asked the Second Continental

Thomas Jefferson (in the red vest) presents the finished Declaration of Independence to the Second Continental Congress in this painting from 1818.

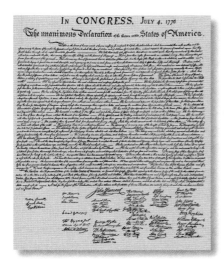

The original Declaration of Independence is in the National Archives in Washington, D.C.

Congress to declare the colonies "free and independent states."

Virginia delegate Thomas Jefferson wrote the first draft of the Declaration. The four other members of the drafting committee were John Adams of Massachusetts, Roger Sherman of Connecticut, Benjamin Franklin of Pennsylvania, and Robert R. Livingston of New York. The Congress made final revisions.

The preamble, or introduction, states the Declaration's purpose and philosophical principles. A list of grievances follows. Each explains why the colonies wanted their freedom. All of that supports the concluding argument, that the "united colonies are, and . . . ought to be free and independent states" and that the "political connection between them and the state of Great Britain, is and ought to be totally dissolved." The government of the new country would be different from any that modern history had seen. It would be for the people and by the people.

The Congress officially adopted the Declaration of Independence at the Pennsylvania statehouse in Philadelphia, on July 4, 1776. Church bells rang out to celebrate the day the Declaration of Independence was accepted. Our country was officially born.

King George III: Hi, Tom! What's up?

Thomas Jefferson: The time has come for us to be free from your rule!

What a bunch of ingrates.

Listen, you need to pay attention to this. We're declaring our independence from Britain. We will no longer be governed by your laws!

Oh, *okay*. Let's have a look-see.

What's all this about aliens?

Not aliens. *Inalienable*. Inalienable rights are rights that cannot be taken away or denied.

You have rights under my rule. How can you think I'm a tyrant?

Do you need to ask? We wrote a list of grievances against you. Look on the next page.

In Congress, July 4, 1776.

The unanimous Declaration of the thirteen united States of America, When in the Course of human events, it becomes necessary for one people to dissolve the political bands which have connected them with another, and to assume among the powers of the earth, the separate and equal station to which the Laws of Nature and of Nature's God entitle them, a decent respect to the opinions of mankind requires that they should declare the causes which impel them to the separation.

We hold these truths to be self-evident, that all men are created equal, that they are endowed by their Creator with certain unalienable Rights, that among these are Life, Liberty and the pursuit of Happiness.—That to secure these rights, Governments are instituted among Men, deriving their just powers from the consent of the governed,—That whenever any Form of Government becomes destructive of these ends, it is the Right of the People to alter or to abolish it, and to institute new Government, laying its foundation on such principles and organizing its powers in such form, as to them shall seem most likely to effect their Safety and Happiness. Prudence, indeed, will dictate that Governments long established should not be changed for light and transient causes; and accordingly all experience hath shewn, that mankind are more disposed to suffer, while evils are sufferable, than to right themselves by abolishing the forms to which they are accustomed. But when a long train of abuses and usurpations, pursuing invariably the same Object evinces a design to reduce them under absolute Despotism, it is their right, it is their duty, to throw off such Government, and to provide new Guards for their future security.—Such has been the patient sufferance of these Colonies; and such is now the necessity which constrains them to alter their former Systems of Government. The history of the present King of Great Britain is a history of repeated injuries and usurpations, all having in direct object the establishment of an absolute Tyranny over these States. To prove this, let Facts be submitted to a candid world.

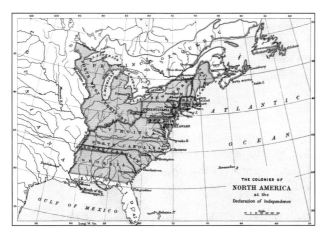

This map shows the United States of America in 1776. Areas in pink are the 13 colonies that broke away from Great Britain.

You don't approve laws that we need. You reject many of them. Others you ignore and neglect.

Our colonies are growing. You refuse to allow these communities to have equal representation in the government.

That's not true. You have councils and assemblies.

That hardly counts. Colonists don't have access to information. They don't know when meetings are or where they will be held.

Well, maybe the colonists need to stop protesting!

You can't keep disbanding our governments because of our protests. This isn't working for us!

He has refused his Assent to Laws, the most wholesome and necessary for the public good.

He has forbidden his Governors to pass Laws of immediate and pressing importance, unless suspended in their operation till his Assent should be obtained; and when so suspended, he has utterly neglected to attend to them.

He has refused to pass other Laws for the accommodation of large districts of people, unless those people would relinquish the right of Representation in the Legislature, a right inestimable to them and formidable to tyrants only.

He has called together legislative bodies at places unusual, uncomfortable, and distant from the depository of their public Records, for the sole purpose of fatiguing them into compliance with his measures.

He has dissolved Representative Houses repeatedly, for opposing with manly firmness his invasions on the rights of the people.

He has refused for a long time, after such dissolutions, to cause others to be elected; whereby the Legislative

And what about this? Our population is small. We need more people to help us grow bigger and more powerful. You are preventing Europeans from migrating to the colonies!

Also, we need our own judicial system.

We have royal courts in the colonies. Isn't that enough?

powers, incapable of Annihilation, have returned to the People at large for their exercise; the State remaining in the mean time exposed to all the dangers of invasion from without, and convulsions within.

He has endeavoured to prevent the population of these States; for that purpose obstructing the Laws for Naturalization of Foreigners; refusing to pass others to encourage their migrations hither, and raising the conditions of new Appropriations of Lands.

He has obstructed the Administration of Justice, by refusing his Assent to Laws for establishing Judiciary powers.

He has made Judges dependent on his Will alone, for the tenure of their offices, and the amount and payment of their salaries.

MEET THE AUTHOR

THOMAS JEFFERSON

Thomas Jefferson was a great thinker, architect, inventor, farmer, and patriot. He served as America's ambassador to France, secretary of state, vice president, and president. During his first term as president, Jefferson made an important decision to expand the territory of the United States. In 1803, he bought a huge area of land from France. The Louisiana Purchase just about doubled the size of America.

After two terms as president, Jefferson returned to Monticello, Virginia. He continued to write until his death on July 4, 1826—50 years after he penned the Declaration of Independence.

While Jefferson was beloved, his legacy is not simple. Although he wrote often about the need to abolish slavery, he himself owned as many as 600 enslaved men, women, and children in his lifetime.

He has erected a multitude of New Offices, and sent hither swarms of Officers to harrass our people, and eat out their substance.

He has kept among us, in times of peace, Standing Armies without the Consent of our legislatures.

He has affected to render the Military independent of and superior to the Civil power.

He has combined with others to subject us to a jurisdiction foreign to our constitution, and unacknowledged by our laws; giving his Assent to their Acts of pretended Legislation:

For Quartering large bodies of armed troops among us:

For protecting them, by a mock Trial, from punishment for any Murders which they should commit on the Inhabitants of these States:

For cutting off our Trade with all parts of the world:

For imposing Taxes on us without our Consent:

For depriving us in many cases, of the benefits of Trial by Jury:

For transporting us beyond Seas to be tried for pretended offences

For abolishing the free System of English Laws in a neighbouring Province, establishing therein an Arbitrary government, and enlarging its Boundaries so as to render it at once an example and fit instrument for introducing the same absolute rule into these Colonies:

For taking away our Charters, abolishing our most valuable Laws, and altering fundamentally the Forms of our Governments:

For suspending our own Legislatures, and declaring themselves invested with power to legislate for us in all cases whatsoever.

And we protect you! We give you soldiers and weapons.

You tax us to pay off your war debt.

Part of that debt comes from protecting YOU from the French.

And about those soldiers . . .

Here we go again . . .

Even in times of peace, there are too many soldiers around. We are forced to let them stay in our homes. They eat our food and sleep in our beds!

AND you closed Boston Harbor. You cut us off from trade with every other part of the world.

You threw 340 chests of tea into the harbor!

Heh-heh. That was a good one.

Look, the fact is that you are not keeping us safe. You declared that you will no longer protect the colonies.

Ugh. So much complaining. Why can't you just follow the rules?

You have burned down many of our towns. You take what you want and do what you want. You have hired foreign troops to come in and fight against us.

It's just some friends helping us out. We need to make sure the colonies are behaving.

You encourage American Indians and enslaved people to fight against us.

Hey, it's a long trip to get to the colonies from Britain. They are helping us keep control.

Benjamin Franklin (left), John Adams (center), and Thomas Jefferson work on the Declaration in this period painting.

He has abdicated Government here, by declaring us out of his Protection and waging War against us.

He has plundered our seas, ravaged our Coasts, burnt our towns, and destroyed the lives of our people.

He is at this time transporting large Armies of foreign Mercenaries to compleat the works of death, desolation and tyranny, already begun with circumstances of Cruelty & perfidy scarcely paralleled in the most barbarous ages, and totally unworthy the Head of a civilized nation.

He has constrained our fellow Citizens taken Captive on the high Seas to bear Arms against their Country, to become the executioners of their friends and Brethren, or to fall themselves by their Hands.

He has excited domestic insurrections amongst us, and has endeavoured to bring on the inhabitants of our frontiers, the merciless Indian Savages, whose known rule of warfare, is an undistinguished destruction of all ages, sexes and conditions.

In every stage of these Oppressions We have Petitioned for Redress in the most humble terms: Our repeated Petitions have been answered only by repeated injury. A Prince whose character is thus marked by every act which may define a Tyrant, is unfit to be the ruler of a free people.

Nor have We been wanting in attentions to our Brittish brethren. We have warned them from time to time of attempts by their legislature to extend an unwarrantable jurisdiction over us. We have reminded them of the circumstances of our emigration and settlement here. We have appealed to their native justice and magnanimity, and we have conjured them by the ties of our common kindred to disavow these usurpations, which, would inevitably interrupt our connections and correspondence. They too have been deaf to the voice of justice and of consanguinity. We must, therefore, acquiesce in the necessity, which denounces our Separation, and hold them, as we hold the rest of mankind, Enemies in War, in Peace Friends.

We, therefore, the Representatives of the united States of America, in General Congress, Assembled, appealing to the Supreme Judge of the world for the rectitude of our intentions, do, in the Name, and by Authority of the good People of these Colonies, solemnly publish and declare, That these United Colonies are, and of Right ought to be Free and Independent States; that they are Absolved from all Allegiance to the British Crown, and that all political connection between them and the State of Great Britain, is and ought to be totally dissolved; and that as Free and Independent States, they have full Power to levy War, conclude Peace, contract Alliances, establish Commerce, and to do all other Acts and Things which Independent States may of right do. And for the support of this Declaration, with a firm reliance on the protection of divine Providence, we mutually pledge to each other our Lives, our Fortunes and our sacred Honor.

We have asked you many times to address our concerns.

Listen, maybe this whole thing has gotten a little out of hand.

We are British subjects, you know.

Maybe we can agree to disagree. Wouldn't it be easier if we all just got along?

I don't think so, George. I think we BOTH know where this is going.

THE U.S. CONSTITUTION

Signed September 17, 1787

Minuteman

T he U.S. Constitution is what makes our country different from most other nations. It lays out the structure of our national government, and it explains how our government works. The Constitution also gives the people who live in our country their rights. One of its key ideas is that all Americans are to be treated fairly and with respect.

The Constitution was written more than 200 years ago, in 1787, at a time when our country was very

George Washington (on pedestal in black) observes the signing of the Constitution in this late 19th-century painting by Thomas P. Rossiter.

new. It replaced the Articles of Confederation, which had been ratified, or approved, by the 13 original colonies in 1781. The Articles had provided a framework for governing the colonies after they won independence from Britain. Under the Articles, each state operated like its own country. The national government was weak and did not even have the power to tax people. That meant there was little money coming in to keep the federal government

The original Constitution is on display at the National Archives in Washington, D.C.

running effectively. The country's leading citizens knew the system was not working and decided to hold a meeting—the Constitutional Convention—to discuss the changes that needed to be made to the government. The meeting took place in Philadelphia, Pennsylvania, starting in May 1787. By early September, there was enough agreement among the representatives that they managed to create the Constitution. Made up of seven Articles, the document described a strong national government that split its power among three branches—legislative, executive, and judicial—with no single branch having more power than the others. The leaders who wrote the Constitution, called the Framers, also knew that the country would face new problems. They included a way to make changes, called amendments, to the Constitution.

The preamble is the opening statement of the Constitution. This short text outlines the general goals of the Framers and the purpose of the Constitution: to create a fair government and to ensure peace for the residents of our country. The very first phrase is "We the people of the United States." This places the government's power in Americans' hands. It means that the nation will be ruled by the people, not a king or dictator. This first phrase shows that the Framers wanted the United States to be one nation—not just a combination of people from different states. The preamble also says that the government will seek to establish justice and be fair, and will provide protection and defense for the country. The preamble is largely the work of one man, Gouverneur Morris, a member of the Pennsylvania delegation to the Constitutional Convention. The convention chose Morris to be part of the Committee of Style. The job of that committee was to produce a final draft of the Constitution and put into clearer language the complicated text the delegates had arrived at during the convention.

Preamble

We the People of the United States, in Order to form a more perfect Union, establish Justice, insure domestic Tranquility, provide for the common defence, promote the general Welfare, and secure the Blessings of Liberty to ourselves and our Posterity, do ordain and establish this Constitution for the United States of America.

Article I lays out the role of Congress. Congress is the legislative branch of government, which means it makes laws. The authors of the Constitution initially had different ideas about how many representatives from each state should be allowed in the government. The leaders reached a compromise by creating a system with two houses: the House of Representatives and the Senate.

Article I explains how representatives and senators will be chosen, and how many of them there will be. The Senate is made up of two senators from each state, while the House of Representatives has representatives from each state based on the state's population. This Article also describes the process of how laws are passed in Congress. It lays out the specific powers of Congress, such as the ability to establish an army, to raise money, and to declare war. Article I also lists some limits on the power of Congress and on individual states.

Many other important institutions in our country were established in Article I. As another way to unify the 13 states into one country, Congress was given the power to issue a national currency. Article I also created a national post office system.

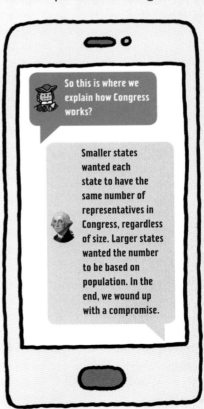

So this is where we explain how Congress works?

Smaller states wanted each state to have the same number of representatives in Congress, regardless of size. Larger states wanted the number to be based on population. In the end, we wound up with a compromise.

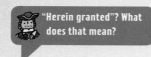

"Herein granted"? What does that mean?

That means Congress has to stick to the powers listed in the Constitution.

No freestyling?

Nope.

I have a bad feeling about this three-fifths thing.

It wasn't our best work. Southern states wanted to count enslaved people. Northern states worried that would give the South too many representatives. They compromised and agreed that each enslaved person would count as three-fifths of a person.

That doesn't sound right.

Nothing's right about saying that someone is less than a whole person.

Article I

Section 1

All legislative Powers herein granted shall be vested in a Congress of the United States, which shall consist of a Senate and House of Representatives.

Section 2

The House of Representatives shall be composed of Members chosen every second Year by the People of the several States, and the Electors in each State shall have the Qualifications requisite for Electors of the most numerous Branch of the State Legislature.

No Person shall be a Representative who shall not have attained to the Age of twenty five Years, and been seven Years a Citizen of the United States, and who shall not, when elected, be an Inhabitant of that State in which he shall be chosen.

Representatives and direct Taxes shall be apportioned among the several States which may be included within this Union, according to their respective Numbers, which shall be determined by adding to the whole Number of free Persons, including those bound to Service for a Term of Years, and excluding Indians not taxed, three fifths of all other Persons. The actual Enumeration shall be made within three Years after the first Meeting of the Congress of the United States, and within every subsequent Term of ten Years, in such Manner as they shall by Law direct. The Number of Representatives shall not exceed one for every thirty Thousand, but each State shall have at Least one Representative; and until such enumeration shall be made, the State of New Hampshire shall be entitled to chuse three, Massachusetts eight, Rhode-Island and Providence Plantations one, Connecticut five, New-York six, New Jersey four, Pennsylvania eight, Delaware one, Maryland six, Virginia ten, North Carolina five, South Carolina five, and Georgia three.

When vacancies happen in the Representation from any State, the Executive Authority thereof shall issue Writs of Election to fill such Vacancies. The House of

Representatives shall chuse their Speaker and other Officers; and shall have the sole Power of Impeachment.

Section 3
The Senate of the United States shall be composed of two Senators from each State, chosen by the Legislature thereof, for six Years; and each Senator shall have one Vote.

Immediately after they shall be assembled in Consequence of the first Election, they shall be divided as equally as may be into three Classes. The Seats of the Senators of the first Class shall be vacated at the Expiration of the second Year, of the second Class at the Expiration of the fourth Year, and of the third Class at the Expiration of the sixth Year, so that one third may be chosen every second Year; and if Vacancies happen by Resignation, or otherwise, during the Recess of the Legislature of any State, the Executive thereof may make temporary Appointments until the next Meeting of the Legislature, which shall then fill such Vacancies.

No Person shall be a Senator who shall not have attained to the Age of thirty Years, and been nine Years a Citizen of the United States, and who shall not, when elected, be an Inhabitant of that State for which he shall be chosen.

The Vice President of the United States shall be President of the Senate, but shall have no Vote, unless they be equally divided.

The Senate shall chuse their other Officers, and also a President pro tempore, in the Absence of the Vice President, or when he shall exercise the Office of President of the United States.

The Senate shall have the sole Power to try all Impeachments. When sitting for that Purpose, they shall be on Oath or Affirmation. When the President of the United States is tried, the Chief Justice shall preside: And no Person shall be convicted without the Concurrence of two thirds of the Members present.

Yum! Peaches!

Peaches are pretty good, but impeachment is serious. Impeaching is the process of bringing charges against a president. Only the House of Representatives can do it.

Okay, so the House brings charges. Then what happens?

The Senate holds a trial.

The Senate can send the president to jail?

Actually, no. The Senate can only remove the president from office. We didn't want the legislative branch to overlap with the judicial branch. Separation of powers is one of the most important features of the Constitution.

Okay, so if elections happen in November, why does the Constitution say that Congress should meet in December?

It takes a long time to travel on horseback across the country. Newly elected officials started their jobs in the following December— one year after their election.

Huh. I hadn't thought of that. If the people from farther away took too long to get to the capital, Congress could just start without them.

Nope. They have to have a quorum. That means a majority of people have to be there to start a session.

That makes sense. But couldn't they just start Congress later and make everyone's lives easier?

They will. That's what the 20th Amendment is for!

The first two sessions of the newly formed U.S. Congress were held at Federal Hall in New York City.

Judgment in Cases of Impeachment shall not extend further than to removal from Office, and disqualification to hold and enjoy any Office of honor, Trust or Profit under the United States: but the Party convicted shall nevertheless be liable and subject to Indictment, Trial, Judgment and Punishment, according to Law.

Section 4

The Times, Places and Manner of holding Elections for Senators and Representatives, shall be prescribed in each State by the Legislature thereof; but the Congress may at any time by Law make or alter such Regulations, except as to the Places of chusing Senators.

The Congress shall assemble at least once in every Year, and such Meeting shall be on the first Monday in December, unless they shall by Law appoint a different Day.

Section 5

Each House shall be the Judge of the Elections, Returns and Qualifications of its own Members, and a Majority of each shall constitute a Quorum to do Business; but a smaller Number may adjourn from day to day, and may be authorized to compel the Attendance of absent

Members, in such Manner, and under such Penalties as each House may provide.

Each House may determine the Rules of its Proceedings, punish its Members for disorderly Behaviour, and, with the Concurrence of two thirds, expel a Member.

Each House shall keep a Journal of its Proceedings, and from time to time publish the same, excepting such Parts as may in their Judgment require Secrecy; and the Yeas and Nays of the Members of either House on any question shall, at the Desire of one fifth of those Present, be entered on the Journal.

Neither House, during the Session of Congress, shall, without the Consent of the other, adjourn for more than three days, nor to any other Place than that in which the two Houses shall be sitting.

Section 6

The Senators and Representatives shall receive a Compensation for their Services, to be ascertained by Law, and paid out of the Treasury of the United States. They shall in all Cases, except Treason, Felony and Breach of the Peace, be privileged from Arrest during their Attendance at the Session of their respective Houses, and in going to and returning from the same; and for any Speech or Debate in either House, they shall not be questioned in any other Place.

No Senator or Representative shall, during the Time for which he was elected, be appointed to any civil Office under the Authority of the United States, which shall have been created, or the Emoluments whereof shall have been encreased during such time; and no Person holding any Office under the United States, shall be a Member of either House during his Continuance in Office.

Section 7

All Bills for raising Revenue shall originate in the House of Representatives; but the Senate may propose or concur with Amendments as on other Bills.

Compensation? You get paid to be in Congress? Sweet!

Yep. Some of the Framers, including Benjamin Franklin, thought that members of Congress should not be paid. But others wanted to make sure that people who weren't wealthy could afford to participate in government.

Hmmm...maybe I should run for Congress.

That's the idea.

Wait a minute. After all that, Congress can't pass a law unless the president says it's okay?

Well, they can, but it's difficult. To overrule the president, two-thirds of the members of the Senate and the House have to vote to do so. It's pretty hard to get two-thirds of Congress to agree on anything.

I don't get it. Why not just let Congress pass the laws they want?

This is probably the most important thing about the Constitution. Each of the three branches of the government is separate from the others. Checks and balances make sure no single branch becomes too powerful.

Okay, so the president can stop Congress from passing unjust laws. And Congress can impeach the president if he's not doing a good job.

Exactly.

Every Bill which shall have passed the House of Representatives and the Senate, shall, before it become a Law, be presented to the President of the United States; If he approve he shall sign it, but if not he shall return it, with his Objections to that House in which it shall have originated, who shall enter the Objections at large on their Journal, and proceed to reconsider it. If after such Reconsideration two thirds of that House shall agree to pass the Bill, it shall be sent, together with the Objections, to the other House, by which it shall likewise be reconsidered, and if approved by two thirds of that House, it shall become a Law. But in all such Cases the Votes of both Houses shall be determined by yeas and Nays, and the Names of the Persons voting for and against the Bill shall be entered on the Journal of each House respectively. If any Bill shall not be returned by the President within ten Days (Sundays excepted) after it shall have been presented to him, the Same shall be a Law, in like Manner as if he had signed it, unless the Congress by their Adjournment prevent its Return, in which Case it shall not be a Law.

Every Order, Resolution, or Vote to which the Concurrence of the Senate and House of Representatives may be necessary (except on a question of Adjournment) shall be presented to the President of the United States; and before the Same shall take Effect, shall be approved by him, or being disapproved by him, shall be repassed by two thirds of the Senate and House of Representatives, according to the Rules and Limitations prescribed in the Case of a Bill.

Section 8

The Congress shall have Power To lay and collect Taxes, Duties, Imposts and Excises, to pay the Debts and provide for the common Defence and general Welfare of the United States; but all Duties, Imposts and Excises shall be uniform throughout the United States;

To borrow Money on the credit of the United States;

To regulate Commerce with foreign Nations, and among the several States, and with the Indian Tribes;

To establish an uniform Rule of Naturalization, and uniform Laws on the subject of Bankruptcies throughout the United States;

To coin Money, regulate the Value thereof, and of foreign Coin, and fix the Standard of Weights and Measures; To provide for the Punishment of counterfeiting the Securities and current Coin of the United States;

To establish Post Offices and post Roads;

To promote the Progress of Science and useful Arts, by securing for limited Times to Authors and Inventors the exclusive Right to their respective Writings and Discoveries;

To constitute Tribunals inferior to the supreme Court;

To define and punish Piracies and Felonies committed on the high Seas, and Offences against the Law of Nations;

To declare War, grant Letters of Marque and Reprisal, and make Rules concerning Captures on Land and Water;

To raise and support Armies, but no Appropriation of Money to that Use shall be for a longer Term than two Years; To provide and maintain a Navy; To make Rules for the Government and Regulation of the land and naval Forces;

To provide for calling forth the Militia to execute the Laws of the Union, suppress Insurrections and repel Invasions;

Whoa! This is kind of a long list. This is all the stuff Congress can collect taxes for?

Yep. Before the Constitution came along, Congress couldn't force states to support the federal government, and things were kind of a mess. The Constitution made sure that the states would provide the federal government with funds for important infrastructure, like post offices and roads.

And an army?

Sort of. After occupation by the British, people were afraid to have a standing army, which could turn a president into a tyrant. So no funding for a federal army could last more than two years. We're counting on local militias and minutemen like you to be ready to fight in an emergency.

I've got your back, GW.

To provide for organizing, arming, and disciplining, the Militia, and for governing such Part of them as may be employed in the Service of the United States, reserving to the States respectively, the Appointment of the Officers, and the Authority of training the Militia according to the discipline prescribed by Congress;

To exercise exclusive Legislation in all Cases whatsoever, over such District (not exceeding ten Miles square) as may, by Cession of particular States, and the Acceptance of Congress, become the Seat of the Government of the United States, and to exercise like Authority over all Places purchased by the Consent of the Legislature of the State in which the Same shall be, for the Erection of Forts, Magazines, Arsenals, dock-Yards, and other needful Buildings;—And

To make all Laws which shall be necessary and proper for carrying into Execution the foregoing Powers, and all other Powers vested by this Constitution in the Government of the United States, or in any Department or Officer thereof.

Section 9

The Migration or Importation of such Persons as any of the States now existing shall think proper to admit, shall not be prohibited by the Congress prior to the Year one thousand eight hundred and eight, but a Tax or duty may be imposed on such Importation, not exceeding ten dollars for each Person.

The Privilege of the Writ of Habeas Corpus shall not be suspended, unless when in Cases of Rebellion or Invasion the public Safety may require it.

No Bill of Attainder or ex post facto Law shall be passed.

No Capitation, or other direct, Tax shall be laid, unless in Proportion to the Census or enumeration herein before directed to be taken.

Uh-oh, I'm getting that bad feeling again . . .

You noticed, huh? Yep, Section 9 includes another reference to slavery. The Constitution never uses the word itself, because anti-slavery delegates were afraid that using the word *slavery* would make it seem legit. But this section says that Congress couldn't do anything to stop slavery before the year 1808. In 1807, Congress passed a law to end the slave trade in 1808.

It's awful that it wasn't sooner.

I agree.

No Tax or Duty shall be laid on Articles exported from any State.

No Preference shall be given by any Regulation of Commerce or Revenue to the Ports of one State over those of another: nor shall Vessels bound to, or from, one State, be obliged to enter, clear, or pay Duties in another.

No Money shall be drawn from the Treasury, but in Consequence of Appropriations made by Law; and a regular Statement and Account of the Receipts and Expenditures of all public Money shall be published from time to time.

No Title of Nobility shall be granted by the United States: And no Person holding any Office of Profit or Trust under them, shall, without the Consent of the Congress, accept of any present, Emolument, Office, or Title, of any kind whatever, from any King, Prince, or foreign State.

Section 10

No State shall enter into any Treaty, Alliance, or Confederation; grant Letters of Marque and Reprisal; coin Money; emit Bills of Credit; make any Thing but gold and silver Coin a Tender in Payment of Debts; pass any Bill of Attainder, ex post facto Law, or Law impairing the Obligation of Contracts, or grant any Title of Nobility.

No State shall, without the Consent of the Congress, lay any Imposts or Duties on Imports or Exports, except what may be absolutely necessary for executing its inspection Laws: and the net Produce of all Duties and Imposts, laid by any State on Imports or Exports, shall be for the Use of the Treasury of the United States; and all such Laws shall be subject to the Revision and Controul of the Congress.

No State shall, without the Consent of Congress, lay any Duty of Tonnage, keep Troops, or Ships of War in time of Peace, enter into any Agreement or Compact with another State, or with a foreign Power, or engage in War, unless actually invaded, or in such imminent Danger as will not admit of delay.

No titles of nobility? Does that mean you can't be king?

That's exactly what it means. After living under British rule, the Continental Congress wanted to make sure that the United States would never again have hereditary aristocracy. Many people were afraid that I would try to become a monarch. They wanted to make sure that never happened!

No lords and ladies?

Nope. And there's also a rule here that says that no one in government can accept a title, office, or gift from foreign kings or governments. That one's going to be in the news a lot later. It's called the emoluments clause.

Article II explains the powers and responsibilities of the president of the United States. When the Constitution was written, its authors were forging into new territory. After years of being ruled by the British monarchy, the Framers knew that they did not want an all-powerful ruler who would serve for life. But beyond that, they disagreed about many of the details. Some believed the president should serve for just two years at a time. Others thought the term should continue for as long as the president showed "good behavior." The Framers decided the president would serve a term of four years, and could be re-elected after each term. After living under the rule of King George III, they wanted to make sure they wouldn't get stuck with a president who was terrible, so they also insisted that the president could face trial in Congress, in a process called impeachment. So far, two presidents have been impeached, Andrew Johnson and Bill Clinton. Neither was found guilty, so they got to keep their jobs.

Article II also lists the president's duties as commander in chief of the armed forces and his obligations to report to Congress.

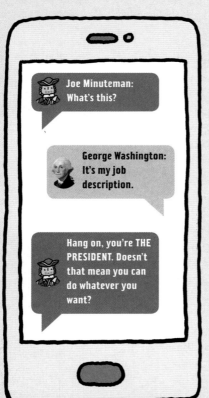

Article II

Section 1

The executive Power shall be vested in a President of the United States of America. He shall hold his Office during the Term of four Years, and, together with the Vice President, chosen for the same Term, be elected, as follows:

Each State shall appoint, in such Manner as the Legislature thereof may direct, a Number of Electors, equal to the whole Number of Senators and Representatives to which the State may be entitled in the Congress: but no Senator or Representative, or Person holding an Office of Trust or Profit under the United States, shall be appointed an Elector.

The Electors shall meet in their respective States, and vote by Ballot for two Persons, of whom one at least shall not be an Inhabitant of the same State with themselves. And they shall make a List of all the Persons voted for, and of the Number of Votes for each; which List they shall sign and certify, and transmit sealed to the Seat of the Government of the United States, directed to the President of the Senate. The President of the Senate shall, in the Presence of the Senate and House of Representatives, open all the Certificates, and the Votes shall then be counted. The Person having the greatest Number of Votes shall be the President, if such Number be a Majority of the whole Number of Electors appointed; and if there be more than one who have such Majority, and have an equal Number of Votes, then the House of Representatives shall immediately chuse by Ballot one of them for President; and if no Person have a Majority, then from the five highest on the List the said House shall in like Manner chuse the President. But in chusing the President, the Votes shall be taken by States, the Representation from each State having one Vote; A quorum for this Purpose shall consist of a Member or Members from two thirds of the States, and a Majority of all the States shall be necessary to a Choice. In every Case, after the Choice of the President, the Person having the greatest Number of Votes of the Electors shall be the Vice President. But if there should remain two or more who have equal Votes, the Senate shall chuse from them by Ballot the Vice President.

The Congress may determine the Time of chusing the Electors, and the Day on which they shall give their Votes; which Day shall be the same throughout the United States.

Hey, this whole voting thing seems a little vague. Can you explain it to me?

Don't worry about it. We're going to fix it in 1804 with the 12th Amendment.

Wait. WHAT? I thought this thing was final.

It's a LIVING document, Joe. That means that we can change things as we go along. You didn't really think we were going to get everything exactly right the first time, did you?

Well, yeah, kind of.

For crying out loud, Joe, it's 1787. We haven't even invented the telephone yet.

No Person except a natural born Citizen, or a Citizen of the United States, at the time of the Adoption of this Constitution, shall be eligible to the Office of President; neither shall any Person be eligible to that Office who shall not have attained to the Age of thirty five Years, and been fourteen Years a Resident within the United States.

In Case of the Removal of the President from Office, or of his Death, Resignation, or Inability to discharge the Powers and Duties of the said Office, the Same shall devolve on the Vice President, and the Congress may by Law provide for the Case of Removal, Death, Resignation or Inability, both of the President and Vice President, declaring what Officer shall then act as President, and such Officer shall act accordingly, until the Disability be removed, or a President shall be elected.

The President shall, at stated Times, receive for his Services, a Compensation, which shall neither be encreased nor diminished during the Period for which he shall have been elected, and he shall not receive within that Period any other Emolument from the United States, or any of them.

Before he enter on the Execution of his Office, he shall take the following Oath or Affirmation:—"I do solemnly swear (or affirm) that I will faithfully execute the Office of President of the United States, and will to the best of my Ability, preserve, protect and defend the Constitution of the United States."

Section 2
The President shall be Commander in Chief of the Army and Navy of the United States, and of the Militia of the several States, when called into the actual Service of the United States; he may require the Opinion, in writing, of the principal Officer in each of the executive Departments, upon any Subject relating to the Duties of their respective Offices, and

What's this about compensation?

It says that Congress can't raise or lower my pay as a way to get me to do what they want. It makes sure that I am able to do what I think is right, instead of what Congress wants me to do.

Section 2 looks cool. You're already a general, so you have a lot of practice with this. Will you be in charge of the Air Force, too?

Airplanes aren't going to be invented until 1903, but future presidents will.

he shall have Power to grant Reprieves and Pardons for Offences against the United States, except in Cases of Impeachment.

He shall have Power, by and with the Advice and Consent of the Senate, to make Treaties, provided two thirds of the Senators present concur; and he shall nominate, and by and with the Advice and Consent of the Senate, shall appoint Ambassadors, other public Ministers and Consuls, Judges of the supreme Court, and all other Officers of the United States, whose Appointments are not herein otherwise provided for, and which shall be established by Law: but the Congress may by Law vest the Appointment of such inferior Officers, as they think proper, in the President alone, in the Courts of Law, or in the Heads of Departments.

The President shall have Power to fill up all Vacancies that may happen during the Recess of the Senate, by granting Commissions which shall expire at the End of their next Session.

Section 3

He shall from time to time give to the Congress Information of the State of the Union, and recommend to their Consideration such Measures as he shall judge necessary and expedient; he may, on extraordinary Occasions, convene both Houses, or either of them, and in Case of Disagreement between them, with Respect to the Time of Adjournment, he may adjourn them to such Time as he shall think proper; he shall receive Ambassadors and other public Ministers; he shall take Care that the Laws be faithfully executed, and shall Commission all the Officers of the United States.

Section 4

The President, Vice President and all civil Officers of the United States, shall be removed from Office on Impeachment for, and Conviction of, Treason, Bribery, or other high Crimes and Misdemeanors.

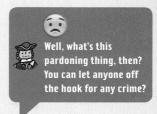

Well, what's this pardoning thing, then? You can let anyone off the hook for any crime?

Pretty much. Unless I'm impeached. Then I'm out of luck.

LOL!

Article III creates the judicial branch of the United States. The first section creates the Supreme Court, the highest court in the country. The Supreme Court has the final say on matters of federal law. Justices are appointed by the president with the approval of the Senate. The Constitution does not specify how many justices there will be on the Supreme Court, but current law says there must be nine, including one chief justice. In addition, this section of the Constitution gives Congress the power to create lower federal courts throughout the country. There are now United States district courts located in every state, and regional United States courts of appeals. This Article also explains the crime of treason, which is described as giving "aid and comfort" to an enemy. Treason is the only crime defined in the Constitution. By defining it, the founders made sure that those accused of treason have to do more than simply say things our government or leaders don't like.

So this is about the Supreme Court? It's kind of short.

There was a lot of disagreement, so the Constitution just set up the highest court. They left everything else to be ironed out later.

As long as I don't have to iron it. I hate housework.

Article III

Section 1

The judicial Power of the United States, shall be vested in one supreme Court, and in such inferior Courts as the Congress may from time to time ordain and establish. The Judges, both of the supreme and inferior Courts, shall hold their Offices during good Behaviour, and shall, at stated Times, receive for their Services, a Compensation, which shall not be diminished during their Continuance in Office.

Section 2

The judicial Power shall extend to all Cases, in Law and Equity, arising under this Constitution, the Laws of the United States, and Treaties made, or which shall be made, under their Authority;—to all Cases affecting Ambassadors, other public Ministers and Consuls;—to all Cases of admiralty and maritime Jurisdiction;—to Controversies to which the United States shall be a Party;—to Controversies between two or more States;—between a State and Citizens of another State,—between Citizens of different States,—between Citizens of the same State claiming Lands under Grants of different States, and between a State, or the Citizens thereof, and foreign States, Citizens or Subjects.

In all Cases affecting Ambassadors, other public Ministers and Consuls, and those in which a State shall be Party, the supreme Court shall have original Jurisdiction. In all the other Cases before mentioned, the supreme Court shall have appellate Jurisdiction, both as to Law and Fact, with such Exceptions, and under such Regulations as the Congress shall make.

The Trial of all Crimes, except in Cases of Impeachment, shall be by Jury; and such Trial shall be held in the State where the said Crimes shall have been committed; but when not committed within any State, the Trial shall be at such Place or Places as the Congress may by Law have directed.

Section 3

Treason against the United States, shall consist only in levying War against them, or in adhering to their Enemies, giving them Aid and Comfort. No Person shall be convicted of Treason unless on the Testimony of two Witnesses to the same overt Act, or on Confession in open Court.

The Congress shall have Power to declare the Punishment of Treason, but no Attainder of Treason shall work Corruption of Blood, or Forfeiture except during the Life of the Person attainted.

Whoa. That's a lot of "cases" and "controversies."

We wanted to make sure that the Supreme Court would only hear cases that come before it—not be used as a legal adviser to the president or Congress. But other than that, there aren't a lot of rules about the Supreme Court in the Constitution. It wasn't until 1803 that the court declared, in a famous case, that it was its job to determine what the law is.

But what about this treason part?

We wanted to make sure the court couldn't be used against political opponents, so we defined treason really carefully.

Okay, but all this blood stuff is a little over the top ...

That just means that if you're convicted of treason, your family members can't be punished along with you.

That seems fair.

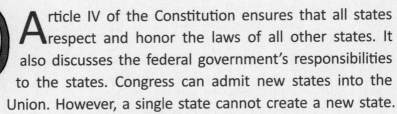

A rticle IV of the Constitution ensures that all states respect and honor the laws of all other states. It also discusses the federal government's responsibilities to the states. Congress can admit new states into the Union. However, a single state cannot create a new state. For example, the state of California can't make the city of Los Angeles a separate state. In addition, Article IV says that the U.S. federal government must guarantee each state a government that is run as a democracy, with power coming from the people. The section also gives Congress the power to protect states from an invasion by a foreign country.

States' rights. I love those! Maybe I'll start my own state. I'll call it Joelandia!

Sorry, Joe. No can do. That's the main point of Article IV.

You're no fun.

Article IV

Section 1

Full Faith and Credit shall be given in each State to the public Acts, Records, and judicial Proceedings of every other State. And the Congress may by general Laws prescribe the Manner in which such Acts, Records and Proceedings shall be proved, and the Effect thereof.

Section 2

The Citizens of each State shall be entitled to all Privileges and Immunities of Citizens in the several States.

A Person charged in any State with Treason, Felony, or other Crime, who shall flee from Justice, and be found in another State, shall on Demand of the executive Authority of the State from which he fled, be delivered up, to be removed to the State having Jurisdiction of the Crime.

No Person held to Service or Labour in one State, under the Laws thereof, escaping into another, shall, in Consequence of any Law or

A political cartoon published in 1754 pushed the colonies to join together as a republic. But each state has individual needs, too.

Regulation therein, be discharged from such Service or Labour, but shall be delivered up on Claim of the Party to whom such Service or Labour may be due.

Section 3

New States may be admitted by the Congress into this Union; but no new State shall be formed or erected within the Jurisdiction of any other State; nor any State be formed by the Junction of two or more States, or Parts of States, without the Consent of the Legislatures of the States concerned as well as of the Congress.

The Congress shall have Power to dispose of and make all needful Rules and Regulations respecting the Territory or other Property belonging to the United States; and nothing in this Constitution shall be so construed as to Prejudice any Claims of the United States, or of any particular State.

Section 4

The United States shall guarantee to every State in this Union a Republican Form of Government, and shall protect each of them against Invasion; and on Application of the Legislature, or of the Executive (when the Legislature cannot be convened), against domestic Violence.

Sorry, Joe. But it was really important that Congress be in charge. When the Constitution was written, there were only 13 states, but we knew the number would grow. In the Wild West, anything could happen. Two states might try to claim the same territory. Or a part of a state might try to break off and form its own separate state. We had to make sure that new states were created in a way that was fair for the states that already existed.

Well, when you put it that way . . .

We did let the states set up their own governments, though. And we promised that we would protect them if they suffered rebellion.

Okay, you won me over. No Joelandia. Maybe I'll just move to Kentucky. I hear it's going to be a state soon.

Article V is one major reason why the Constitution has stood the test of time. The Framers knew that the U.S. Constitution would sometimes need to be changed. Article V establishes the process for amending, or changing, it. After an amendment is officially proposed, it first needs to be approved by two-thirds of both houses of Congress. Then it needs to be approved by three-quarters, or 75 percent, of the states. By allowing for amendments, the Framers made sure that the Constitution would be able to adapt to changing times.

Article V

The Congress, whenever two thirds of both Houses shall deem it necessary, shall propose Amendments to this Constitution, or, on the Application of the Legislatures of two thirds of the several States, shall call a Convention for proposing Amendments, which, in either Case, shall be valid to all Intents and Purposes, as Part of this Constitution, when ratified by the Legislatures of three fourths of the several States, or by Conventions in three fourths thereof, as the one or the other Mode of Ratification may be proposed by the Congress; Provided that no Amendment which may be made prior to the Year One thousand eight hundred and eight shall in any Manner affect the first and fourth Clauses in the Ninth Section of the first Article; and that no State, without its Consent, shall be deprived of its equal Suffrage in the Senate.

Individual states had acquired a lot of debt during the Revolutionary War. Article VI makes it clear that the new government established by the Constitution could be counted on to repay debt. This section also says that when state law is in conflict with federal law, federal law must prevail. Article VI states that both federal and state officials must obey the U.S. Constitution. This Article also ensures freedom of religion, and is the only place in the main text of the Constitution that refers to religion. In Britain at that time, religious tests were used to exclude from office anyone who was not a member of the Church of England. This section of the Constitution says that no religious tests are required for anyone who wants to run for a federal office. Article VII details the method for ratification, or acceptance, of the Constitution. It took two and a half years for all the states to ratify the Constitution.

Article VI

All Debts contracted and Engagements entered into, before the Adoption of this Constitution, shall be as valid against the United States under this Constitution, as under the Confederation.

This Constitution, and the Laws of the United States which shall be made in Pursuance thereof; and all Treaties made, or which shall be made, under the Authority of the United States, shall be the supreme Law of the Land; and the Judges in every State shall be bound thereby, any Thing in the Constitution or Laws of any State to the Contrary notwithstanding.

The Senators and Representatives before mentioned, and the Members of the several

Looks like we're down to the small details.

They may look small, but they're important. The Framers didn't want to give Congress the power to veto state laws. They'd been there before. But they needed to make sure that the federal government has the final word.

State Legislatures, and all executive and judicial Officers, both of the United States and of the several States, shall be bound by Oath or Affirmation, to support this Constitution; but no religious Test shall ever be required as a Qualification to any Office or public Trust under the United States.

Article VII

The Ratification of the Conventions of nine States, shall be sufficient for the Establishment of this Constitution between the States so ratifying the Same.

Attest
William Jackson,
Secretary

MEET THE AUTHOR

JAMES MADISON

James Madison, the son of a Virginia plantation owner, was a small man who was often sick. He felt that he was too weak to hold an important job. But Madison was a strong thinker and an expert on British laws. When the American colonies finally broke away from Britain, Madison knew that the new country would need a government strong enough to protect people's rights, but not so strong that it could take away people's freedom. He was just the person to help. He wrote many parts of the Constitution, including what became the Bill of Rights. Then he did something even more difficult: he helped persuade people to accept it.

Madison served as secretary of state when Thomas Jefferson was president. Then Madison became president in 1809. France and Britain were still fighting a war. The U.S. was caught in the middle. When the British attacked American ships, Madison felt it was time to fight back. The War of 1812 lasted two and a half years. In the end, the war was seen as an American victory, and Madison left office as a popular president.

done in Convention by the Unanimous Consent of the States present the Seventeenth Day of September in the Year of our Lord one thousand seven hundred and Eighty seven and of the Independance of the United States of America the Twelfth. In witness whereof We have hereunto subscribed our Names,

George Washington
President and deputy from Virginia

Delaware
Geo: Read
Gunning Bedford jun
John Dickinson
Richard Bassett
Jaco: Broom

Maryland
James McHenry
Dan of St Thos. Jenifer
Danl. Carroll

Virginia
John Blair
James Madison Jr.

North Carolina
Wm. Blount
Richd. Dobbs Spaight
Hu. Williamson

South Carolina
J. Rutledge
Charles Cotesworth
    Pinckney
Charles Pinckney
Pierce Butler

Georgia
William Few
Abr Baldwin

New Hampshire
John Langdon
Nicholas Gilman

Massachusetts
Nathaniel Gorham
Rufus King

Connecticut
Wm. Saml. Johnson
Roger Sherman

New York
Alexander Hamilton

New Jersey
Wil: Livingston
David Brearley
Wm. Paterson
Jona: Dayton

Pennsylvania
B. Franklin
Thomas Mifflin
Robt. Morris
Geo. Clymer
Thos. FitzSimons
Jared Ingersoll
James Wilson
Gouv. Morris

 WHOA! Look at all these guys. There are some big names here!

 Recognize anyone?

 YEAH! You're at the top.

 I was the president of the Constitutional Convention. I made sure things flowed smoothly. (Later on, I got to be president of the United States, too!)

 Hey, Benjamin Franklin was there, too! And Alexander Hamilton!

 Ummmm...weren't we talking about me?

 Look—Gouverneur Morris! That guy wrote a mean preamble.

 Ugh. Maybe it's time to wrap this up.

The Constitution established a strong national government and explained the rights of the states. But it did not include any discussion about the rights of the people who live in our country. The absence of a "bill of rights" prevented the Constitution from being approved by all states. After George Washington was elected as our country's first president in 1789, he asked the newly elected Congress to consider adding the rights of citizens to the Constitution. James Madison, one of the Framers of the Constitution, worked on a list. Madison used the list of rights from his own state, Virginia, to come up with ideas. He also drew inspiration from the Magna Carta, an important document in England that put limits on the powers of the king. Madison initially proposed 17 amendments. The Senate and the House of Representatives debated them, and finally came up with a list of 12. These were sent to the states for final ratification, and after a two-year process, 10 amendments were decided on. In 1791, the Bill of Rights became part of the U.S. Constitution. It puts limits on what the U.S. government can do. The Bill of Rights originally protected only land-owning white men. It did not provide the same protection for women or African Americans. It took more constitutional amendments and Supreme Court cases to give the same rights to all American citizens.

Colonial woman

The Amendments

Congress of the United States begun and held at the City of New-York, on Wednesday the fourth of March, one thousand seven hundred and eighty nine.

The Conventions of a number of the States, having at the time of their adopting the Constitution, expressed a desire, in order to prevent misconstruction or abuse of its powers, that further declaratory and restrictive clauses should be added: And as extending the ground of public confidence in the Government, will best ensure the beneficent ends of its institution.

Resolved by the Senate and House of Representatives of the United States of America, in Congress assembled, two thirds of both Houses concurring, that the following Articles be proposed to the Legislatures of the several States, as amendments to the Constitution of the United States, all, or any of which Articles, when ratified by three fourths of the said Legislatures, to be valid to all intents and purposes, as part of the said Constitution; viz.

Articles in addition to, and Amendment of the Constitution of the United States of America, proposed by Congress, and ratified by the Legislatures of the several States, pursuant to the fifth Article of the original Constitution.

A painting from 1790 shows Quakers at a meeting. Before the passage of the Bill of Rights, the Quakers, a Christian group, were often persecuted for their beliefs.

 So, what is the Bill of Rights?

 It's a list of amendments that protect the rights of the people.

 The amendments make up the Bill of Rights?

 Yes, there are ten.

 There are ten amendments?

 No, there are 27 amendments.

 That doesn't make any sense!

 The first ten amendments were all ratified at once. They are called the Bill of Rights. The rest were added one at a time.

 I get it! But what's the bill for? I thought rights were free!

 I think you'd better let me ask the questions, Joe.

The First Amendment has many important ideas. It prevents the government from setting up an official religion for the country. Many early settlers in the 13 colonies had traveled to the United States to escape religious persecution. At the time, many European countries allowed one religion only, and prohibited the practice of others. The First Amendment also says that people are entitled to freedom of speech. That means that people in the United States can speak openly about what they think and feel. They can criticize the government without fear of getting punished. The First Amendment also protects the freedom of assembly. This can mean physically gathering with a group of people to protest something. It can also mean associating with other people in groups for political or religious reasons. Another important protection Americans get from the First Amendment is freedom of the press. It prevents the government from passing any laws that block access to information. Although this amendment originally applied to newspapers, leaflets, and books, in modern times it also includes television and the internet.

Amendment I

Congress shall make no law respecting an establishment of religion, or prohibiting the free exercise thereof; or abridging the freedom of speech, or of the press; or the right of the people peaceably to assemble, and to petition the Government for a redress of grievances.

The Second Amendment is one of the most controversial parts of the Bill of Rights, because its language has been interpreted in different ways. It says that, "A well regulated Militia, being necessary to the security of a free State, the right of the people to keep and bear Arms, shall not be infringed." The Supreme Court interpreted this to mean that individuals have the right to own weapons under certain circumstances but that government can regulate them in some ways. Gun control laws help keep track of guns and determine what types of weapons people are allowed to own. Individual states also have their own gun laws. All 50 states have some limitations on the sale and manufacture of weapons, but laws vary widely from state to state.

The Third Amendment says that members of the military cannot stay in private homes without permission from the owners. It's unlikely that soldiers would need to stay in someone's home today. But this amendment remains important, because it protects people's right to ownership of their property without government interference.

Amendment II

A well regulated Militia, being necessary to the security of a free State, the right of the people to keep and bear Arms, shall not be infringed.

Amendment III

No Soldier shall, in time of peace be quartered in any house, without the consent of the Owner, nor in time of war, but in a manner to be prescribed by law.

So this second amendment...

I guess we could've written it better. A lot of people in the future are going to disagree about what it means.

You really should've amended your amendment.

The Fourth Amendment provides protection for people from searches and seizures by government officials. A search can be anything from a police officer looking at what's in your car to federal agents entering your home. People in our country are protected from being searched without a reason. Law officers must have either probable cause to believe that something illegal is taking place or permission from a judge before searching anyone. The Fourth Amendment also protects people from unlawful seizure. This means the government can't take control of a person's possessions without a reason. Seized property can be used as evidence when an individual is charged with a crime. But if a search or seizure is judged to be in violation of the Fourth Amendment, the evidence can't be used in a trial against the person.

The Fifth Amendment ensures that someone in our country who is accused of a federal crime must be brought before a jury of ordinary citizens. The job of the jury is to determine if the government has enough evidence to bring any charges. This amendment also protects people from being forced to reveal to the police, prosecutors, judges, or jury members any information that might lead to their own criminal prosecution. The Fifth Amendment ensures that prosecutors need to come up with evidence to prove their cases. This is the foundation of the very important idea in our legal system that you are innocent until proven guilty.

So no one can come into my house without a really good reason?

Nope. Not even the police.

What if I called them?

Well, that's a really good reason.

Amendment IV

The right of the people to be secure in their persons, houses, papers, and effects, against unreasonable searches and seizures, shall not be violated, and no Warrants shall issue, but upon probable cause, supported by Oath or affirmation, and particularly describing the place to be searched, and the persons or things to be seized.

Amendment V

No person shall be held to answer for a capital, or otherwise infamous crime, unless on a presentment or indictment of a Grand Jury, except in cases arising in the land or naval forces, or in the Militia, when in actual service in time of War or public danger; nor shall any person be subject for the same offence to be twice put in jeopardy of life or limb; nor shall be compelled in any criminal case to be a witness against himself, nor be deprived of life, liberty, or property, without due process of law; nor shall private property be taken for public use, without just compensation.

I love *Jeopardy!* It's too bad you can't play it twice!

It's a different kind of jeopardy, Joe. It means that once you've been acquitted of a crime, you can't be tried for it again.

You also don't have to say anything if you think it will get you into trouble. In 1966, the Supreme Court ruled that police have to inform people of this right. The court case was called *Miranda v. Arizona*, so the right to remain silent has come to be known as one of the Miranda rights.

What do you think of that, Joe?

What? No jokes?

Shhhh ... I'm exercising my Miranda rights.

In colonial America, British troops carried writs of assistance, which gave them permission to search any home. Here, patriot James Otis is depicted leaving the courthouse after arguing against the rule.

The Sixth Amendment provides many protections and rights to a person accused of a crime. One of these rights is for a person to have his or her case heard in a public trial by an impartial jury. This is an independent group of people from the surrounding community who are willing to decide the case based only on the evidence. This right is considered one of the most important in the Constitution. Without it, a criminal defendant could be held indefinitely under a cloud of unproven criminal accusations. The amendment also guarantees the right to a speedy trial, which means that the government cannot hold someone accused of a crime for long periods of time. If too much time elapses between the alleged crime and the trial, witnesses may leave the area, their memories may fade, and physical evidence may be lost.

The Sixth Amendment also gives criminal defendants the right to be present at their trials, to question the witnesses who testify against them, and to have lawyers represent them at trial.

The Seventh Amendment refers to noncriminal, or civil, cases. These are cases such as car accidents, arguments over land, and issues that come up in the workplace. This amendment says that all people have the right to trial by jury in cases in which they go to court to settle disputes about property or money.

> It seems like there are a lot of amendments that protect criminals.

> They protect *everyone*. Dictators often use the courts and jails to suppress political enemies. These amendments are designed to ensure that people are tried or imprisoned only for valid reasons.

Amendment VI

In all criminal prosecutions, the accused shall enjoy the right to a speedy and public trial, by an impartial jury of the State and district wherein the crime shall have been committed, which district shall have been previously ascertained by law, and to be informed of the nature and cause of the accusation; to be confronted with the witnesses against him; to have compulsory process for obtaining witnesses in his favor, and to have the Assistance of Counsel for his defence.

Amendment VII

In Suits at common law, where the value in controversy shall exceed twenty dollars, the right of trial by jury shall be preserved, and no fact tried by a jury, shall be otherwise re-examined in any Court of the United States, than according to the rules of the common law.

Those accused of criminal and civil offenses have the right to a trial by jury.

See? Amendment VI guarantees the right to a speedy trial. Otherwise, someone who has been accused of a crime could be locked up for long periods even if he or she is innocent.

That sounds like a good thing.

The amendment also makes sure that a case is tried in the same place where the alleged crime occurred. Sending a person far away for trial can cause hardship and make it difficult to organize a proper defense.

Amendment VII might also sound a little strange, but it means that a civil case has to be heard by a jury, and the second half of the amendment is really important. It says that once a jury has come to a verdict, the courts have to respect it. A jury verdict can't be overturned or changed by a judge, either.

POWER TO THE PEOPLE!

You bet.

The Eighth Amendment deals with punishment. It says that the government cannot give harsh punishments to people convicted of crimes. It can't charge people high fees to get released from prison before they stand trial, or charge unfair fines as punishments for crimes. This amendment is intended to ensure that a criminal defendant's punishment is not out of proportion with the seriousness of the crime itself.

The Ninth Amendment does not refer to any specific rights. It is meant to make clear that people have other rights than those that are listed in the First through Eighth Amendments. These unspecified rights are referred to as "unenumerated." The Supreme Court has found that unenumerated rights include the right to travel and the rights to keep personal matters private and to make important decisions about one's health care or body.

What's emu-meration?

To be *enumerated* is to be specifically listed.

What do emus have to do with it?

Nothing, Joe. There are no emus anywhere in the Constitution.

Amendment VIII

Excessive bail shall not be required, nor excessive fines imposed, nor cruel and unusual punishments inflicted.

Amendment IX

The enumeration in the Constitution, of certain rights, shall not be construed to deny or disparage others retained by the people.

The Tenth Amendment was added to help better define the power balance between the federal government and the states. This amendment says that the federal government has only the powers given to it by the Constitution. Those are the powers that are listed in the Articles. They include the power to collect taxes and declare war. According to the Tenth Amendment, any power not listed is left to the states or the people. This amendment does not specify what those powers may be. Local or state governments sometimes try to say that they do not have to follow some federal laws because of the Tenth Amendment. The U.S. Supreme Court has said that laws affecting families—such as those about adoption and divorce—should be determined by the states or the people. Although there have been periods when the Supreme Court has relied on the Tenth Amendment to strike down federal laws, overall, this amendment has not been used to oppose federal power.

Amendment X

The powers not delegated to the United States by the Constitution, nor prohibited by it to the States, are reserved to the States respectively, or to the people.

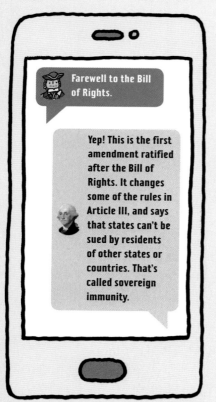

The 11th Amendment, ratified in 1795, was the first amendment to the Constitution after the Bill of Rights. This amendment explains the kinds of cases that the newly created federal courts could hear. It came about after the U.S. Supreme Court ruled in 1793 that it could hear a case brought against the state of Georgia by a citizen of South Carolina. The amendment has been interpreted to mean that U.S. courts cannot hear a case against a state if the state is sued by someone from another state or country. States are also protected from being sued unless they give permission or the federal government gives permission. Protecting states from certain types of legal responsibility is a concept known as sovereign immunity.

Amendment XI

Passed by Congress: March 4, 1794
Ratified: February 7, 1795

The Judicial power of the United States shall not be construed to extend to any suit in law or equity, commenced or prosecuted againstone of the United States by Citizens of another State, or by Citizens or Subjects of any Foreign State.

The 12th Amendment, ratified in 1804, changed the way that the Electoral College chooses the president and vice president. In the original Constitution, the president was the candidate who received the most electoral votes in the Electoral College. The vice president was the candidate who received the second-highest number of electoral votes. That meant that the president and vice president could be from different political parties and have very different ideas about governing. The 12th Amendment allows for there to be a team, or "ticket," that consists of the president and the vice president. This amendment also specifies how the president and vice president are to be chosen if neither candidate obtains the votes of a majority of the electors, and says that the eligibility requirements to become president apply to the vice president as well. This is because no person can be vice president who is unable to be president.

Amendment XII

Passed by Congress: December 9, 1803
Ratified: June 15, 1804

The Electors shall meet in their respective states and vote by ballot for President and Vice-President, one of whom, at least, shall not be an inhabitant of the same state with themselves; they shall name in their ballots the person voted for as President, and in distinct ballots the person voted for as Vice-President, and they shall make distinct lists of all persons voted for as President, and of all persons voted for as Vice-President, and of the number of votes for each, which lists they shall sign and certify, and transmit sealed to the seat of the government of the United States, directed to the President of the Senate;—the President of

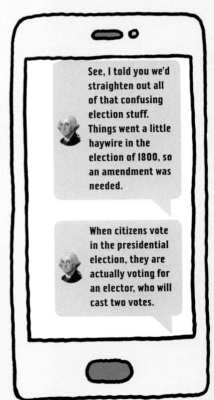

See, I told you we'd straighten out all of that confusing election stuff. Things went a little haywire in the election of 1800, so an amendment was needed.

When citizens vote in the presidential election, they are actually voting for an elector, who will cast two votes.

Wait. What? Why can't I just vote directly for president?

We didn't think that many citizens were qualified to choose the president. Back then, a lot of people couldn't even read.

But we assumed that the electors would vote for candidates based on their qualifications. When the political parties formed, electors started pledging to vote for the candidates from particular parties.

In 1800, all the Republican electors cast their two votes for the two Republican candidates. Thomas Jefferson and Aaron Burr both got the same number of votes, so it was clear that system needed to change.

I still think it should've changed so that I could vote directly for a candidate—so everyone's vote matters the same.

This campaign banner is from the presidential election of 1800. A tie vote led to the passage of the 12th Amendment.

the Senate shall, in the presence of the Senate and House of Representatives, open all the certificates and the votes shall then be counted;—The person having the greatest number of votes for President, shall be the President, if such number be a majority of the whole number of Electors appointed; and if no person have such majority, then from the persons having the highest numbers not exceeding three on the list of those voted for as President, the House of Representatives shall choose immediately, by ballot, the President. But in choosing the President, the votes shall be taken by states, the representation from each state having one vote; a quorum for this purpose shall consist of a member or members from two-thirds of the states, and a majority of all the states shall be necessary to a choice. And if the House of Representatives shall not choose a President whenever the right of choice shall devolve upon them, before the fourth day of March next following, then the Vice-President shall act as President, as in case of the death or other constitutional disability of the President.

The person having the greatest number of votes as Vice-President, shall be the Vice-President, if such number be a majority of the whole number of Electors appointed, and if no person have a majority, then from the two highest numbers on the list, the Senate shall choose the Vice-President; a quorum for the purpose shall consist of two-thirds of the whole number of Senators, and a majority of the whole number shall be necessary to a choice. But no person constitutionally ineligible to the office of President shall be eligible to that of Vice-President of the United States.

ABOLISHING SLAVERY

The 13th Amendment, ratified in 1865 after the Civil War ended, outlawed slavery everywhere in the United States. Slavery was part of our country long before the American Revolution. Before this amendment was adopted, there were many laws that protected states that wanted to maintain slavery. This amendment made slavery illegal in the United States, and prevents anyone from holding slaves. It gives Congress the power to pass laws against slavery and punish people who buy and sell other human beings. This amendment also prohibits involuntary servitude, or the forcing of people to work against their free will, even if they are paid for their labor. After the 13th Amendment was passed, no one could force anyone else to work against their will.

Amendment XIII

Passed by Congress: January 31, 1865
Ratified: December 6, 1865

Section 1

Neither slavery nor involuntary servitude, except as a punishment for crime whereof the party shall have been duly convicted, shall exist within the United States, or any place subject to their jurisdiction.

Section 2

Congress shall have power to enforce this article by appropriate legislation.

EQUAL RIGHTS

The 14th Amendment, ratified in 1868, is one of the most important and powerful sections of the Constitution. This amendment protects the rights of all United States citizens and gives equal protection to all Americans. Before this amendment was added, African Americans were not considered full citizens. At the time when it was proposed, there were many African Americans who had been freed from slavery. Even though they were no longer enslaved, their rights were limited. This amendment granted full citizenship to formerly enslaved people. The 14th Amendment also gives citizenship to people who are born in the United States to parents who are not U.S. citizens. Once someone has American citizenship, it cannot be taken away by Congress or other authorities. This amendment also created new limits on the power of states and gave new protections under the Constitution. Before this amendment, the protections outlined in the Bill of Rights limited the actions of only the federal government. The Supreme Court has since interpreted this amendment to apply to local governments as well. The equal protection section of this amendment specifically limits the ability of states to discriminate against people based on their race, national origin, gender, or other status. This clause has been used to prevent discrimination at jobs and in schools.

Equal rights! Finally, I get to vote!

Errrr…no. Sorry. But we'll get to women in later amendments.

Sigh. Okay, carry on…

Amendment XIV

Passed by Congress: June 13, 1866
Ratified: July 9, 1868

Section 1

All persons born or naturalized in the United States, and subject to the jurisdiction thereof, are citizens of the United States and of the State wherein they reside. No State shall make or enforce any law which shall abridge the privileges or immunities of citizens of the United States; nor shall any State deprive any person of life, liberty, or property, without due process of law; nor deny to any person within its jurisdiction the equal protection of the laws.

Section 2

Representatives shall be apportioned among the several States according to their respective numbers, counting the whole number of persons in each State, excluding Indians not taxed. But when the right to vote at any election for the choice of electors for President and Vice-President of the United States, Representatives in Congress, the Executive and Judicial officers of a State, or the members of the Legislature thereof, is denied to any of the male inhabitants of such State, being twenty-one years of age, and citizens of the United States, or in any way abridged, except for participation in rebellion, or other crime, the basis of representation therein shall be reduced in the proportion which the number of such male citizens shall bear to the whole number of male citizens twenty-one years of age in such State.

Section 3

No person shall be a Senator or Representative in Congress, or elector of President and Vice-President, or hold any office, civil or military, under the United States, or under any State, who, having previously taken an oath, as a member of Congress, or as an officer of the United States, or as a member of any State legislature, or as an executive or judicial officer of any State, to support the Constitution of the United States, shall have engaged in insurrection or rebellion

Okay, so anybody born in the United States is a citizen.

Yes. And all citizens share the same rights.

That seems kind of obvious, doesn't it?

Maybe it does now, but even after slavery was abolished, many freed people weren't considered full citizens. Section 1 made it clear that they should be treated as full citizens. And Section 2 finally got rid of that terrible three-fifths compromise. It counted every taxpaying resident as a whole person.

It's about time!

against the same, or given aid or comfort to the enemies thereof. But Congress may by a vote of two-thirds of each House, remove such disability.

Section 4

The validity of the public debt of the United States, authorized by law, including debts incurred for payment of pensions and bounties for services in suppressing insurrection or rebellion, shall not be questioned. But neither the United States nor any State shall assume or pay any debt or obligation incurred in aid of insurrection or rebellion against the United States, or any claim for the loss or emancipation of any slave; but all such debts, obligations and claims shall be held illegal and void.

Section 5

The Congress shall have the power to enforce, by appropriate legislation, the provisions of this article.

The 14th Amendment gave the federal government the authority to step in and protect Ruby Bridges when she became the first African-American student to attend an all-white school in Louisiana in 1960.

So what about Section 5? That one doesn't seem to say much.

That one's the most important of all. It gives the federal government the right to step in and make sure that states honor the civil rights of their citizens.

That sounds important.

It is. The section has been interpreted a lot of different ways, but in the end it made sure the government could enforce desegregation laws during the Civil Rights Movement. It helped Ruby Bridges go to school and Rosa Parks sit wherever she wanted on the bus.

Whoa? Sixteen words can really do all that?

Yep, they really can.

The 15th Amendment, ratified in 1870, protects the rights of Americans of all races to vote in elections. Before this amendment, African Americans, even those who were not enslaved, couldn't vote. This amendment prohibits the use of race to determine who can vote and how they vote. It puts the voting rights of freed people directly into the Constitution. However, even after this amendment was ratified, many Southern states found ways to prevent black citizens from voting. They used measures such as literacy tests and poll taxes and sometimes even violent acts to prevent African Americans from voting. It wasn't until the Voting Rights Act of 1965 that the right to vote was fully ensured for people of all races.

Amendment XV

Passed by Congress: February 26, 1869
Ratified: February 3, 1870

Section 1
The right of citizens of the United States to vote shall not be denied or abridged by the United States or by any State on account of race, color, or previous condition of servitude.

Section 2
The Congress shall have the power to enforce this article by appropriate legislation.

This amendment made sure that African-American men had the right to vote, even if they had previously been enslaved.

But not African-American women?

Sorry, no.

The 16th Amendment, ratified in 1913, allows the U.S. government to collect an income tax from all Americans. Income tax is money paid to the federal government. It is charged on income, the money that a person earns by working at a job or from a business or rental property. Since this amendment became part of the Constitution, the federal government has collected taxes from Americans every year. These funds are used to build roads and bridges and enforce laws.

Amendment XVI

Passed by Congress: July 2, 1909
Ratified: February 3, 1913

The Congress shall have power to lay and collect taxes on incomes, from whatever source derived, without apportionment among the several States, and without regard to any census or enumeration.

Not everyone was thrilled about the idea of paying income tax to the federal government. A political cartoon from 1900 shows an American taxpayer so poor that he has no clothes to wear.

So there was no federal income tax until the 1900s?

Yep, Article I of the Constitution gave Congress the right to tax states, but not individual people.

But what did candidates talk about when they ran for president?

The 17th Amendment, ratified in 1913, ensures that voters directly choose senators. There are two senators for every state, and 100 in total. Prior to this amendment, voters did not elect senators. State legislators elected them. There was widespread corruption in this process, which meant that people were often using favors or their own wealth to help get them into office. This amendment made sure that any person who could vote in a state election could also vote for the senators in that state.

Amendment XVII

Passed by Congress: May 13, 1912
Ratified: April 8, 1913

The Senate of the United States shall be composed of two Senators from each State, elected by the people thereof, for six years; and each Senator shall have one vote. The electors in each State shall have the qualifications requisite for electors of the most numerous branch of the State legislatures.

When vacancies happen in the representation of any State in the Senate, the executive authority of such State shall issue writs of election to fill such vacancies: Provided, That the legislature of any State may empower the executive thereof to make temporary appointments until the people fill the vacancies by election as the legislature may direct.

This amendment shall not be so construed as to affect the election or term of any Senator chosen before it becomes valid as part of the Constitution.

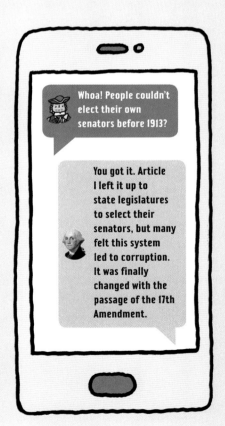

Whoa! People couldn't elect their own senators before 1913?

You got it. Article I left it up to state legislatures to select their senators, but many felt this system led to corruption. It was finally changed with the passage of the 17th Amendment.

TEMPERANCE

The 18th Amendment, ratified in 1919, prohibited the making and sale of alcohol. The temperance movement was a decades-long crusade against alcohol. The supporters of this movement believed that the use of alcohol was destructive and that a prohibition of alcohol would reduce crime and help improve the health of Americans. But prohibiting alcohol had consequences as well. An illegal trade in alcohol flourished, giving rise to famous gangsters such as Al Capone. The 18th Amendment eventually became the first and only constitutional amendment to be repealed.

Amendment XVIII

Passed by Congress: December 18, 1917
Ratified: January 16, 1919

Section 1
After one year from the ratification of this article the manufacture, sale, or transportation of intoxicating liquors within, the importation thereof into, or the exportation thereof from the United States and all territory subject to the jurisdiction thereof for beverage purposes is hereby prohibited.

Section 2
The Congress and the several States shall have concurrent power to enforce this article by appropriate legislation.

Section 3
This article shall be inoperative unless it shall have been ratified as an amendment to the Constitution by the legislatures of the several States, as provided in the Constitution, within seven years from the date of the submission hereof to the States by the Congress.

The 19th Amendment, ratified in 1920, gave women the right to vote. For much of America's history, women—along with African Americans—did not have the right to vote. The fight for women's rights was called the suffrage movement, and it began in the 1840s. This movement lasted through much of the late 19th and early 20th century. An amendment to give the vote to women was first introduced in 1878, but it failed to get through Congress. Supporters of women's right to vote then turned their attention to states. Before the 19th Amendment was ratified, many states, including New York and most Western states, had already given women the right to vote, and some women had even been elected to office. After working for many years to get their amendment through Congress, the suffragettes finally succeeded with the 19th Amendment. This amendment ensured that women in the U.S. have all the same rights as men when it comes to voting. It dramatically expanded the number of people who could vote in our country.

Amendment XIX

Passed by Congress: June 4, 1919
Ratified: August 18, 1920

The right of citizens of the United States to vote shall not be denied or abridged by the United States or by any State on account of sex.

Congress shall have power to enforce this article by appropriate legislation.

The 20th Amendment, ratified in 1933, allows for a quicker transition for new presidents and members of Congress. It moves up the time when the new Congress begins its session, from March to early January. When the Constitution was written, members of Congress needed time to settle their affairs at home and travel to Washington. As transportation and communication improved, it was no longer necessary for there to be so much time built in before new members took office. This amendment also moves the date of the presidential inauguration from March to January. That shortens the time that a president who has not been re-elected remains in office before his or her successor takes over. This amendment also makes clear that the vice president elect will become president if the president-elect should die before taking office.

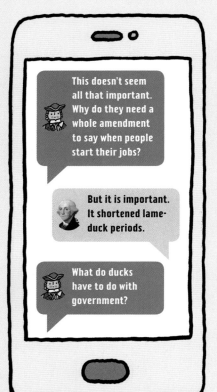

This doesn't seem all that important. Why do they need a whole amendment to say when people start their jobs?

But it is important. It shortened lame-duck periods.

What do ducks have to do with government?

Amendment XX

Passed by Congress: March 2, 1932
Ratified: January 23, 1933

Section 1
The terms of the President and the Vice President shall end at noon on the 20th day of January, and the terms of Senators and Representatives at noon on the 3d day of January, of the years in which such terms would have ended if this article had not been ratified; and the terms of their successors shall then begin.

Section 2
The Congress shall assemble at least once in every year, and such meeting shall begin at noon on the 3d day of January, unless they shall by law appoint a different day.

Franklin Delano Roosevelt takes the oath of office in January 1933.

Section 3

If, at the time fixed for the beginning of the term of the President, the President elect shall have died, the Vice President elect shall become President. If a President shall not have been chosen before the time fixed for the beginning of his term, or if the President elect shall have failed to qualify, then the Vice President elect shall act as President until a President shall have qualified; and the Congress may by law provide for the case wherein neither a President elect nor a Vice President elect shall have qualified, declaring who shall then act as President, or the manner in which one who is to act shall be selected, and such person shall act accordingly until a President or Vice President shall have qualified.

Section 4

The Congress may by law provide for the case of the death of any of the persons from whom the House of Representatives may choose a President whenever the right of choice shall have devolved upon them, and for the case of the death of any of the persons from whom the Senate may choose a Vice President whenever the right of choice shall have devolved upon them.

Section 5

Sections 1 and 2 shall take effect on the 15th day of October following the ratification of this article.

Section 6

This article shall be inoperative unless it shall have been ratified as an amendment to the Constitution by the legislatures of three-fourths of the several States within seven years from the date of its submission.

Ducks don't have anything to do with government.

Then why are you trying to make them shorter?

Lame ducks, Joe. Not actual ducks. A lame duck is an elected official who has been voted out of office but is finishing up his or her term.

What's wrong with them, then?

Well, lame ducks aren't worried about re-election and they know that their jobs will be over soon. They don't have as many reasons to do a good job.

I guess I get that.

The 21st Amendment was ratified in 1933, and it returned the right to regulate alcohol to the states. After the 18th Amendment was ratified in 1919, the country spent 14 years in Prohibition. During that time, alcohol was not allowed to be made, sold, or transported. Federal, state, and local law enforcement was overwhelmed by the effort required to enforce this ban. Underground criminal groups began to provide alcohol to people who wanted it. Prohibition was considered a massive failure. This amendment allows states to set their own rules about how alcohol is sold and imported. Now laws on alcohol sales vary from state to state. This is the first and only amendment that specifically eliminates another amendment to the Constitution.

Amendment XXI

Passed by Congress: February 20, 1933
Ratified: December 5, 1933

Section 1
The eighteenth article of amendment to the Constitution of the United States is hereby repealed.

Section 2
The transportation or importation into any State, Territory, or possession of the United States for delivery or use therein of intoxicating liquors, in violation of the laws thereof, is hereby prohibited.

Section 3
This article shall be inoperative unless it shall have been ratified as an amendment to the Constitution by conventions in the several States, as provided in the Constitution, within seven years from the date of the submission hereof to the States by the Congress.

The 22nd Amendment, ratified in 1951, limits an elected president to two terms, or eight years, in office. The nation's first president, George Washington, was president for two terms. His two-term limit became the unwritten rule for all presidents until Franklin Delano Roosevelt. Roosevelt ran for four terms. Following his death, Congress pushed to make the two-term limit a requirement in the Constitution. It is possible for a president to serve for up to ten years. If the vice president or other successor takes over and serves two years or less of the former president's term, the new president may then be elected to two full four-year terms.

Amendment XXII

Passed by Congress: March 21, 1947
Ratified: February 27, 1951

Section 1

No person shall be elected to the office of the President more than twice, and no person who has held the office of President, or acted as President, for more than two years of a term to which some other person was elected President shall be elected to the office of the President more than once. But this Article shall not apply to any person holding the office of President when this Article was proposed by the Congress, and shall not prevent any person who may be holding the office of President, or acting as President, during the term within which this Article becomes operative from holding the office of President or acting as President during the remainder of such term.

Section 2

This article shall be inoperative unless it shall have been ratified as an amendment to the Constitution by the legislatures of three-fourths of the several States within seven years from the date of its submission to the States by the Congress.

The 23rd Amendment, ratified in 1961, gives the people in the District of Columbia the right to vote. New York City was the nation's first capital, and then the capital was moved to Philadelphia for ten years. In 1800, the District of Columbia (D.C.) became the official seat of government. It was considered a federal territory. At first, there weren't many people who lived there. But by 1960, when this amendment was passed, there were more than 700,000 residents in D.C. This amendment gives residents there the right to have their votes counted in presidential elections. However, this amendment did not give residents of D.C. representation in Congress. D.C. has a delegate who can speak from the floor, but this person cannot vote on the final passage of legislation.

Amendment XXIII

Passed by Congress: June 16, 1960
Ratified: March 29, 1961

Section 1
The District constituting the seat of Government of the United States shall appoint in such manner as the Congress may direct: A number of electors of President and Vice President equal to the whole number of Senators and Representatives in Congress to which the District would be entitled if it were a State, but in no event more than the least populous State; they shall be in addition to those appointed by the States, but they shall be considered, for the purposes of the election of President and Vice President, to be electors appointed by a State; and they shall meet in the District and perform such duties as provided by the twelfth article of amendment.

Section 2
The Congress shall have power to enforce this article by appropriate legislation.

The 24th Amendment, ratified in 1964, removed poll taxes, which were state fees that some citizens had to pay in order to vote. These taxes and other requirements had been put in place in Southern states to keep African Americans from voting. Earlier amendments had granted voting rights to African Americans and had eliminated most discriminatory laws. But poll taxes still discriminated against black citizens, who were less likely to be able to afford them. The removal of these fees was seen as a way to ensure that all people in America would be able to vote.

Amendment XXIV

Passed by Congress: August 27, 1962
Ratified: January 23, 1964

Section 1
The right of citizens of the United States to vote in any primary or other election for President or Vice President, for electors for President or Vice President, or for Senator or Representative in Congress, shall not be denied or abridged by the United States or any State by reason of failure to pay any poll tax or other tax.

Section 2
The Congress shall have power to enforce this article by appropriate legislation.

The 25th Amendment, ratified in 1967, makes it clear what happens when a president dies in office, leaves the office, or is disabled and cannot serve. Article II, Section 1 of the Constitution states that the vice president will carry out the duties of the president if something happens to the president while in office. This amendment makes it clear that the vice president becomes president in the event of the president's death or removal. It came about because at several times in our country's history, the president has died while in office. One president, Richard M. Nixon, resigned and stepped down from the presidency.

Amendment XXV

Passed by Congress: July 6, 1965
Ratified: February 10, 1967

Section 1
In case of the removal of the President from office or of his death or resignation, the Vice President shall become President.

Section 2
Whenever there is a vacancy in the office of the Vice President, the President shall nominate a Vice President who shall take office upon confirmation by a majority vote of both Houses of Congress.

Section 3
Whenever the President transmits to the President pro tempore of the Senate and the Speaker of the House of Representatives his written declaration that he is unable to discharge the powers and duties of his office, and until he transmits to them a written declaration to the

contrary, such powers and duties shall be discharged by the Vice President as Acting President.

Section 4

Whenever the Vice President and a majority of either the principal officers of the executive departments or of such other body as Congress may by law provide, transmit to the President pro tempore of the Senate and the Speaker of the House of Representatives their written declaration that the President is unable to discharge the powers and duties of his office, the Vice President shall immediately assume the powers and duties of the office as Acting President.

Thereafter, when the President transmits to the President pro tempore of the Senate and the Speaker of the House of Representatives his written declaration that no inability exists, he shall resume the powers and duties of his office unless the Vice President and a majority of either the principal officers of the executive department or of such other body as Congress may by law provide, transmit within four days to the President pro tempore of the Senate and the Speaker of the House of Representatives their written declaration that the President is unable to discharge the powers and duties of his office. Thereupon Congress shall decide the issue, assembling within forty-eight hours for that purpose if not in session. If the Congress, within twenty-one days after receipt of the latter written declaration, or, if Congress is not in session, within twenty-one days after Congress is required to assemble, determines by two-thirds vote of both Houses that the President is unable to discharge the powers and duties of his office, the Vice President shall continue to discharge the same as Acting President; otherwise, the President shall resume the powers and duties of his office.

But didn't Article II cover all this?

Not really. Article II says that when a president is killed or otherwise incapacitated, the vice president will discharge the duties of the president, but it wasn't really clear what that meant. This amendment made it clear that the vice president doesn't just carry out the president's duties. The vice president BECOMES the president.

That's a pretty big difference.

It sure is, and if the vice president becomes the president, you need rules about who becomes the vice president, too.

VOTING AGE

The 26th Amendment, ratified in 1971, gave more people the right to vote. This amendment gives voting rights to young adults ages 18 and up. When the Constitution was ratified in 1788, most states limited voting to white males who were over the age of 21. In 1970, Congress amended the Voting Rights Act of 1965 to give the right to vote to Americans who were at least 18 years old. However, those voting rights applied only to federal elections. This amendment applied those changes to state elections as well. It was passed during the Vietnam War. At that time, many Americans between the ages of 18 and 21 were required to join the military and fight for our country. Many people felt that if Americans were old enough to serve in the military, then they should also have the right to vote. Now, when someone turns 18, he or she can vote in all state and federal elections.

Amendment XXVI

Passed by Congress: March 23, 1971
Ratified: July 1, 1971

Section 1
The right of citizens of the United States, who are eighteen years of age or older, to vote shall not be denied or abridged by the United States or by any State on account of age.

Section 2
The Congress shall have power to enforce this article by appropriate legislation.

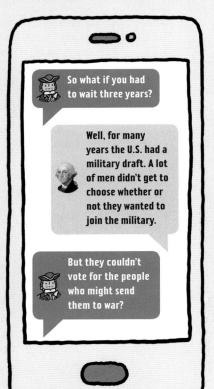

So what if you had to wait three years?

Well, for many years the U.S. had a military draft. A lot of men didn't get to choose whether or not they wanted to join the military.

But they couldn't vote for the people who might send them to war?

★ PAY RAISES

The 27th Amendment, ratified in 1992, prevents members of Congress from giving themselves pay raises during the current session. Any raises that are approved won't take effect until after the next members of Congress have been voted in. It took this amendment over 200 years to find its way into the Constitution. It was first proposed in 1789 by James Madison, but it failed to be ratified at that time. In the early 1990s, Congress had given itself a number of pay raises. There was public frustration with the repeated pay increases. By the spring of 1992, 41 states had approved the amendment and it became part of the Constitution. Many amendments to the Constitution include a time limit for ratification by the states. This amendment did not contain a limit, which is why it could be approved so many years after it was proposed.

Amendment XXVII

Passed by Congress: September 25, 1789
Ratified: May 7, 1992

No law, varying the compensation for the services of the Senators and Representatives, shall take effect, until an election of Representatives shall have intervened.

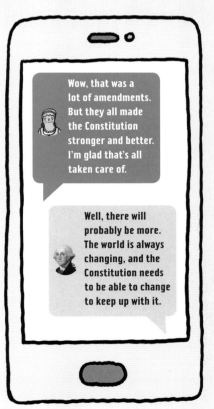

Wow, that was a lot of amendments. But they all made the Constitution stronger and better. I'm glad that's all taken care of.

Well, there will probably be more. The world is always changing, and the Constitution needs to be able to change to keep up with it.

THE MONROE DOCTRINE

Delivered December 2, 1823

John Quincy Adams

In 1823, the United States was growing. Just 20 years earlier, the Louisiana Purchase had doubled the size of the country. New factories were being built in an effort to reduce the country's dependence on foreign goods.

During his State of the Union address, President James Monroe gave a speech that laid out a new policy for how the rapidly changing country would deal with European powers. This set of beliefs came to be known as the Monroe Doctrine, and it was the foundation of U.S. foreign policy for much of the 19th and 20th centuries.

James Monroe (center) and John Quincy Adams (far left) discuss the Monroe Doctrine with the cabinet in this painting by Clyde Deland.

This is the final draft of Monroe's speech to Congress.

In the speech, which he had written with the help of Secretary of State John Quincy Adams, Monroe called on European nations not to interfere in wars or internal affairs in North and South America. He also said that America would stay out of European affairs, and would not interfere with existing colonies in the Western Hemisphere. At that time, many countries in Latin America had recently gained their independence from European powers. The U.S. wanted to ensure that European countries would not seek to reassert control of these regions. Monroe said that the United States would view any effort by Europe to interfere in the Americas as "dangerous to our peace and safety," and he warned that the U.S. would intervene if necessary. The speech also included a warning to Russia, which had been making territorial claims in Canada.

The Monroe Doctrine had a long-lasting impact on American foreign policy. It was invoked several times by U.S. presidents, including Theodore Roosevelt and John F. Kennedy.

This means we can't interfere in European affairs, either.

 What if there is a war in Europe? They are always fighting about something.

We will remain neutral. We have to focus on building our own country.

At the proposal of the Russian Imperial Government, made through the minister of the Emperor residing here, a full power and instructions have been transmitted to the minister of the United States at St. Petersburg to arrange by amicable negotiation the respective rights and interests of the two nations on the northwest coast of this continent. A similar proposal has been made by His Imperial Majesty to the Government of Great Britain, which has likewise been acceded to. The Government of the United States has been desirous by this friendly proceeding of manifesting the great value which they have invariably attached to the friendship of the Emperor and their solicitude to cultivate the best understanding with his Government. In the discussions to which this interest has given rise and in the arrangements by which they

MEET THE AUTHOR

JAMES MONROE

When Thomas Jefferson was president, he sent James Monroe to France to discuss the territory called Louisiana. Monroe helped Jefferson buy the land in the Louisiana Purchase.

Monroe had a distinguished career. He served as governor of Virginia, U.S. senator, diplomat to Britain and France, secretary of state, and secretary of war. When he ran for president in 1816, he won easily.

When Monroe was president, more changes to the U.S. took place. On the western edge of the nation, Missouri wanted to enter the Union as a slavehold-ing state. This was controversial. Finally, in 1820, an agreement called the Missouri Compromise was reached. It allowed Maine to enter as a free state and Missouri as a slaveholding state.

In 1819, Monroe agreed to purchase Florida from Spain. Then, in 1823, he gave his important speech to Congress, outlining the Monroe Doctrine.

After his presidency, he moved home to Virginia and then to New York. He died in New York in 1831.

A political cartoon from 1901 depicts the U.S. as a rooster using the Monroe Doctrine to defend its yard—more than 75 years after the doctrine was written.

may terminate the occasion has been judged proper for asserting, as a principle in which the rights and interests of the United States are involved, that the American continents, by the free and independent condition which they have assumed and maintain, are henceforth not to be considered as subjects for future colonization by any European powers . . .

It was stated at the commencement of the last session that a great effort was then making in Spain and Portugal to improve the condition of the people of those countries, and that it appeared to be conducted with extraordinary moderation. It need scarcely be remarked that the results have been so far very different from what was then anticipated. Of events in that quarter of the globe, with which we have so much intercourse and from which we derive our origin, we have always been anxious and interested spectators. The citizens of the United States cherish sentiments the most friendly in favor of the liberty and happiness of their fellow-men on that side of the Atlantic. In the wars of the European powers in matters relating to themselves we have never taken any part, nor does it comport with our policy to do so. It is only when our rights are invaded or seriously menaced that we resent injuries or make preparation for our defense. With the movements in this hemisphere we are of necessity more immediately connected, and by causes which must be obvious to all enlightened

 Czar Alexander I: Hey, JQA! What's up?

 Hi, Al! Not much. Working on a new doctrine with the boss. What's up with you?

 We just claimed more territory in North America. We're gonna expand our holdings along the northwest coast.

 Not sure that's going to fly, Al. That territory is still being explored.

 What's the big deal? We already have some land there. We are exporting furs and minerals from the West. We want more, just as you do!

In this 1902 cartoon, Venezuela taunts England and Germany, knowing that the Monroe Doctrine will protect it.

Hey, James, have you seen what's going on in Latin America? We are an inspiration! Spanish colonies are becoming independent countries. We need to support them.

Yes, we do. But European countries want to colonize those countries again if they can. How can we protect them? We don't have very much military power ourselves.

We can support them in other ways. We can increase trade with them. We will help them figure out how to govern themselves, just as we have.

and impartial observers. The political system of the allied powers is essentially different in this respect from that of America. This difference proceeds from that which exists in their respective Governments; and to the defense of our own, which has been achieved by the loss of so much blood and treasure, and matured by the wisdom of their most enlightened citizens, and under which we have enjoyed unexampled felicity, this whole nation is devoted. We owe it, therefore, to candor and to the amicable relations existing between the United States and those powers to declare that we should consider any attempt on their part to extend their system to any portion of this hemisphere as dangerous to our peace and safety. With the existing colonies or dependencies of any European power we have not interfered and shall not interfere. But with the Governments who have declared their independence and maintain it, and whose independence we have, on great consideration and on just principles, acknowledged, we could not view any interposition for the purpose of oppressing them, or controlling in any other manner their destiny, by any European power in any other light than as the manifestation of an unfriendly disposition toward the United States. In the war between those new Governments and Spain we declared our neutrality at the time of their recognition, and to this we have adhered, and shall continue to adhere, provided no change shall occur which, in the judgement of the competent authorities of this Government, shall make a corresponding change on the part of the United States indispensable to their security.

The late events in Spain and Portugal shew that Europe is still unsettled. Of this important fact no stronger proof can be adduced than that the allied powers should have thought it proper, on any principle satisfactory to themselves, to have interposed by force in the internal concerns of Spain. To what extent such interposition may be carried, on the same principle, is a question in which all independent powers whose governments differ from theirs are interested, even those most remote, and surely none of them more so than the United States. Our policy in regard to Europe, which was adopted at an early stage of the wars which have so long agitated that quarter of the globe, nevertheless remains the same, which is, not to interfere in the internal concerns of any of its powers; to consider the government de facto as the legitimate government for us; to cultivate friendly relations with it, and to preserve those relations by a frank, firm, and manly policy, meeting in all instances the just claims of every power, submitting to injuries from none. But in regard to those continents circumstances are eminently and conspicuously different.

It is impossible that the allied powers should extend their political system to any portion of either continent without endangering our peace and happiness; nor can anyone believe that our southern brethren, if left to themselves, would adopt it of their own accord. It is equally impossible, therefore, that we should behold such interposition in any form with indifference. If we look to the comparative strength and resources of Spain and those new Governments, and their distance from each other, it must be obvious that she can never subdue them. It is still the true policy of the United States to leave the parties to themselves, in hope that other powers will pursue the same course.

We do need to maintain good relations with Britain.

Yes, but we don't want Britain—or anyone else—interfering in our affairs.

The British are also trading heavily with Latin America. They want to issue a joint statement opposing European intervention in the New World.

Britain has its reasons for wanting to join with us on this one. But we can speak only for ourselves.

At least the British navy will back us up.

What a difference 40 years makes, huh?

THE EMANCIPATION PROCLAMATION

Signed January 1, 1863

Frederick Douglass

When President Abraham Lincoln signed the Emancipation Proclamation on January 1, 1863, he changed the course of the country. This document marked the beginning of the end of slavery.

The Emancipation Proclamation freed enslaved people in Southern states that had seceded from the Union. When the Proclamation was signed, the U.S. was in the middle of the Civil War, with Northern states fighting Southern states. The North and the South were deeply divided over many issues, particularly states' rights and slavery. Tensions

Abraham Lincoln (third from left) composes the first draft of the Emancipation Proclamation with his cabinet on July 22, 1862.

The original Proclamation, in Abraham Lincoln's handwriting, is stored at the National Archives in Washington, D.C.

were rising when Lincoln, who opposed slavery, was elected president on November 6, 1860. By May 1861, 11 Southern states had seceded to form the Confederate States of America, where slavery would remain in place. Lincoln was determined to keep the Union from breaking apart, even though it meant war with the South.

At the start of the Civil War in 1861, the Union Army fought to keep the country together. With the signing of the Emancipation Proclamation, Lincoln added the end of slavery as one of the main goals of the war. His decision to issue the document came after months of debate. Ultimately, he decided that slavery must end or the United States—a nation created under the idea that "all men are created equal"— would not survive. Frederick Douglass, a famous abolitionist, responded to the proclamation in a speech, saying, "Everybody is liberated."

Lincoln knew that only Congress could pass a constitutional amendment to outlaw slavery throughout the nation. He played a major role in the passage of the 13th Amendment, which permanently abolished slavery in the country.

Lincoln did not live to see it ratified. He was assassinated on April 14, 1865, just days after the Confederacy surrendered. But he had set the U.S. on the path to freedom and equality for all.

I was born enslaved, as you know. I taught myself how to read. I escaped to New York.

I know all about you, Mr. Douglass. You are a leading black spokesman in our country. You campaign tirelessly for the freedom of enslaved people.

We are now entering the third year of the Civil War. Enslaved people are helping the Confederate cause! They are working in armories and factories to aid the war effort in the South. We need to have black soldiers fighting for the Union in this war. Black men want to volunteer as soldiers for the Union. I know they can help win this war.

I agree. It is a military necessity to free enslaved people in the South. We need them to help the Union.

An artist's imagining of a Union soldier reading the Proclamation to a group of enslaved people.

January 1, 1863
by the President of the United States of America:

A Proclamation.

Whereas, on the twenty-second day of September, in the year of our Lord one thousand eight hundred and sixty-two, a proclamation was issued by the President of the United States, containing, among other things, the following, to wit:

"That on the first day of January, in the year of our Lord one thousand eight hundred and sixty-three, all persons held as slaves within any State or designated part of a State, the people whereof shall then be in rebellion against the United States, shall be then, thenceforward, and forever free; and the Executive Government of the United States, including the military and naval authority thereof, will recognize and maintain the freedom of such persons, and will do no act or acts to repress such persons, or any of them, in any efforts they may make for their actual freedom.

"That the Executive will, on the first day of January aforesaid, by proclamation, designate the States and parts of States, if any, in which the people thereof, respectively, shall then be in rebellion against the United States; and the fact that any State, or the people thereof, shall on that day be, in good faith, represented in the Congress of the United States by members chosen thereto at elections wherein a majority of the qualified voters of such State shall have participated, shall, in the absence of strong countervailing testimony, be deemed conclusive evidence that such State, and the people thereof, are not then in rebellion against the United States."

Now, therefore I, Abraham Lincoln, President of the United States, by virtue of the power in me vested as Commander-in-Chief, of the Army and Navy of the United States in time of actual armed rebellion against the authority and government of the United States, and as a fit and necessary war measure for suppressing said rebellion, do, on this first day of January, in the year of our Lord one thousand eight hundred and sixty-three, and in accordance with my purpose so to do publicly proclaimed for the full period of one hundred days, from the day first above mentioned, order and designate as the States and parts of States wherein the people thereof respectively, are this day in rebellion against the United States, the following, to wit:

What took you so long to make this proclamation?

Well, I originally planned not to interfere with slavery.

What made you change your mind?

I have always hated slavery. But I was bound by the Constitution.

I still don't understand why you changed your mind.

Thousands of enslaved people in the South are running away to the North. We need a federal policy for how to deal with them.

This is also a moral issue. If we have the sin of slavery, people can never have equality.

That's true, too. I have also come to believe that slavery is a moral issue.

Freedmen gather for work at a coal wharf in Alexandria, Virginia, around 1865.

FREEDOM TO SLAVES!

Whereas, the President of the United States did, on the first day of the present month, issue his *Proclamation* declaring "that all persons held as Slaves in certain designated States, and parts of States, are, and henceforward shall be free," and that the Executive Government of the United States, including the Military and Naval authorities thereof, would recognize and maintain the freedom of said persons. And Whereas, the county of Frederick is included in the territory designated by the Proclamation of the President, in which the Slaves should become free, I therefore hereby notify the citizens of the city of Winchester, and of said County, of said Proclamation, and of my intention to maintain and enforce the same.

I expect all citizens to yield a ready compliance with the Proclamation of the Chief Executive, and I admonish all persons disposed to resist its peaceful enforcement, that upon manifesting such disposition by acts, they will be regarded as rebels in arms against the lawful authority of the Federal Government and dealt with accordingly.

All persons liberated by said Proclamation are admonished to abstain from all violence, and immediately betake themselves to useful occupations.

The officers of this command are admonished and ordered to act in accordance with said proclamation and to yield their ready co-operation in its enforcement.

R. H. Milroy,
Brig. Gen'l Commanding.

Winchester Va.
Jan. 5th, 1863.

This printed notice from the local commander of the Union Army was distributed in Winchester, Virginia, on January 5, 1863.

So, I notice that this proclamation doesn't affect enslaved people in *all* states.

It applies to enslaved people in the Southern states that are in rebellion.

What about the slave-holding border states: Delaware, Kentucky, Maryland, and Missouri?

Okay, you got me. It does not affect enslaved people in those border states. The Union can't risk losing their support.

Well, does it affect enslaved people in Southern areas under Union control?

Ummm...no. This proclamation does not apply to enslaved people in those states, either.

Arkansas, Texas, Louisiana, (except the Parishes of St. Bernard, Plaquemines, Jefferson, St. John, St. Charles, St. James Ascension, Assumption, Terrebonne, Lafourche, St. Mary, St. Martin, and Orleans, including the City of New Orleans) Mississippi, Alabama, Florida, Georgia, South Carolina, North Carolina, and Virginia, (except the forty-eight counties designated as West Virginia, and also the counties of Berkley, Accomac, Northampton, Elizabeth City, York, Princess Ann, and Norfolk, including the cities of Norfolk and Portsmouth[)], and which excepted parts, are for the present, left precisely as if this proclamation were not issued.

And by virtue of the power, and for the purpose aforesaid, I do order and declare that all persons held as slaves within said designated States, and parts of States, are, and henceforward shall be free; and that the Executive government of the United States, including the military and naval authorities thereof, will recognize and maintain the freedom of said persons.

And I hereby enjoin upon the people so declared to be free to abstain from all violence, unless in necessary self-defence; and I recommend to them that, in all cases when allowed, they labor faithfully for reasonable wages.

And I further declare and make known, that such persons of suitable condition, will be received into the armed service of the United States to garrison forts, positions, stations, and other places, and to man vessels of all sorts in said service.

And upon this act, sincerely believed to be an act of justice, warranted by the Constitution, upon military necessity, I invoke the considerate judgment of mankind, and the gracious favor of Almighty God.

In witness whereof, I have hereunto set my hand and caused the seal of the United States to be affixed.

Done at the City of Washington, this first day of January, in the year of our Lord one thousand eight hundred and sixty three, and of the Independence of the United States of America the eighty-seventh.

By the President: ABRAHAM LINCOLN

Okay, maybe it's not perfect, but this proclamation changes everything. The Southern states rely on slavery for their survival. Now enslaved people will join the Union war effort and fight against their masters. The Union cause is now tied directly to the elimination of slavery.

It is a bold action. There is no going back!

ABRAHAM LINCOLN

Abraham Lincoln was born in Kentucky. He had almost no schooling but taught himself to read and write. As a young man, he became a lawyer and was elected to the Illinois state legislature and the U.S. House of Representatives.

In 1860, Lincoln was elected president. Within months, 11 states had left the Union. The Civil War that followed took the lives of more than 600,000 Americans.

In early 1863, Lincoln signed the Emancipation Proclamation. This act emboldened enslaved people, who had already begun to desert their owners. About 200,000 of these freedmen went north to fight in the war.

On April 9, 1865, Robert E. Lee, the Confederate general, surrendered to U.S. general Ulysses S. Grant. Five days later, Lincoln and his wife, Mary, went to see a play. At Ford's Theatre, an actor named John Wilkes Booth shot the president. Lincoln died the next morning.

THE 14 POINTS

Delivered January 8, 1918

At the beginning of 1918, World War I was coming to an end. With the help of 150 advisers, President Woodrow Wilson wrote a speech arguing that more than military victory was needed to secure peace and democracy in the world. On January 18, 1918, he gave his speech to Congress, outlining his plan. The list of proposals became known as the 14 Points.

Some of Wilson's proposals attempted to eliminate the causes of war. He advocated for free trade among countries and a worldwide reduction in weapons and

U.S. soldier, WWI

French prime minister Georges Clemenceau (left), U.S. president Woodrow Wilson (second from right), and British prime minister David Lloyd George leave the Palace of Versailles after signing the treaty that ended World War I.

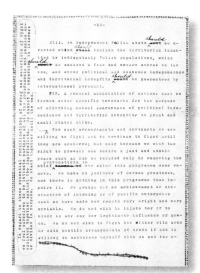

A draft of the speech

armies. He proposed open diplomacy in Europe instead of secret agreements. Other points focused on restoring specific territories occupied during the war. He also said he did not want to punish other countries after the war. Finally, Wilson laid out a vision for a governing body of nations to help secure true peace.

Wilson did not achieve most of the goals he outlined in the 14 Points speech. When the Allied leaders met in Versailles, France, in 1919 to work on the terms of peace after World War I, other leaders did not support many of Wilson's ideas. The leaders of Britain, France, and Italy were interested in regaining what they had lost and also wanted to punish Germany for its role in the war. Ultimately, most of Wilson's 14 points were not included in the treaty. However, Wilson's proposal calling for a world organization that would provide a system of international security was incorporated into the Treaty of Versailles. But the League of Nations faced opposition in the U.S. Senate, and the U.S. did not join the organization.

In 1919, President Wilson was given the Nobel Peace Prize for his efforts to establish peace in Europe and around the world. And after World War II, the United Nations was formed.

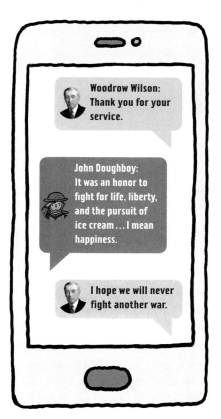

Woodrow Wilson:
Thank you for your service.

John Doughboy:
It was an honor to fight for life, liberty, and the pursuit of ice cream... I mean happiness.

I hope we will never fight another war.

Thank you, Mr. President. I am looking forward to going home and I want to ask that you do something about the horrible army food we had to eat.

I can't do anything about the army food at this moment, but what I can do is outline a plan to secure peace and democracy in the world.

Go on with the "programme" ... I'm listening. I'll make the popcorn.

We entered this war reluctantly. What we want out of it is for the world to be made fit and safe to live in. We're all in this together.

It will be our wish and purpose that the processes of peace, when they are begun, shall be absolutely open and that they shall involve and permit henceforth no secret understandings of any kind. The day of conquest and aggrandizement is gone by; so is also the day of secret covenants entered into in the interest of particular governments and likely at some unlooked-for moment to upset the peace of the world. It is this happy fact, now clear to the view of every public man whose thoughts do not still linger in an age that is dead and gone, which makes it possible for every nation whose purposes are consistent with justice and the peace of the world to avow now or at any other time the objects it has in view.

We entered this war because violations of right had occurred which touched us to the quick and made the life of our own people impossible unless they were corrected and the world secure once for all against their recurrence. What we demand in this war, therefore, is nothing peculiar to ourselves. It is that the world be made fit and safe to live in; and particularly that it be made safe for every peace-loving nation which, like our own, wishes to live its own life, determine its own institutions, be assured of justice and fair dealing by the other peoples of the world as against force and selfish aggression. All the peoples of the world are in effect partners in this interest, and for our own part we see very clearly that unless justice be done to others it will not be done to us. The programme of the world's peace,

MEET THE AUTHOR

WOODROW WILSON

Woodrow Wilson was president from 1913 to 1921. He helped establish shorter workdays, pass child labor laws, and assist farmers with getting loans. After World War I, Wilson wanted to ensure fair terms of peace with his 14 Points. He fought to establish the League of Nations. In 1919, he suffered a stroke. Wilson was seldom seen in public for the remainder of his second term.

therefore, is our programme; and that programme, the only possible programme, as we see it, is this:

I. Open covenants of peace, openly arrived at, after which there shall be no private international understandings of any kind but diplomacy shall proceed always frankly and in the public view.

II. Absolute freedom of navigation upon the seas, outside territorial waters, alike in peace and in war, except as the seas may be closed in whole or in part by international action for the enforcement of international covenants.

III. The removal, so far as possible, of all economic barriers and the establishment of an equality of trade conditions among all the nations consenting to the peace and associating themselves for its maintenance.

IV. Adequate guarantees given and taken that national armaments will be reduced to the lowest point consistent with domestic safety.

V. A free, open-minded, and absolutely impartial adjustment of all colonial claims, based upon a strict observance of the principle that in determining all such questions of sovereignty the interests of the populations concerned must have equal weight with the equitable claims of the government whose title is to be determined.

VI. The evacuation of all Russian territory and such a settlement of all questions affecting Russia as will secure the best and freest cooperation of the other nations of the world in obtaining for her an unhampered and unembarrassed opportunity for the independent determination of her own political development and national policy and assure her of a sincere welcome into the society of free nations under institutions of her own choosing; and, more than a welcome, assistance also of every kind that she may need and may herself desire. The treatment accorded Russia by her sister nations in the months to come will be the acid test of

So you're basically making a blueprint for world peace?

Exactly. Here's the plan: First, no treaties. And ESPECIALLY no secret treaties. Next, international waters should be free to navigate at all times. And I want free trade, too.

Instead of expensive trade?

No, free trade is the exchange of goods and services without high taxes or restrictions. It's a good thing. I am also asking the leaders of each nation to reduce their weapon stores and armies so that more soldiers like you don't lose their lives.

Why would you want to vacuum Russia?

Evacuate. That means we'll pull our troops out of Russia. Belgium, too.

Belgian waffles are my favorite. Of course, they won't be invented until 1958, at the Brussels World's Fair.

Are you listening to me? I have seven more points to make.

I guess I should just stick with ice cream.

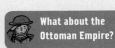

Moving on ... France shall regain all of its lost territory, including the disputed land of Alsace-Lorraine that was conquered by Prussia in 1871. The Central Powers must evacuate Romania, Serbia, and Montenegro, too.

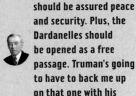

What about the Ottoman Empire?

The Turkish people should be assured peace and security. Plus, the Dardanelles should be opened as a free passage. Truman's going to have to back me up on that one with his doctrine (see page 94).

their good will, of their comprehension of her needs as distinguished from their own interests, and of their intelligent and unselfish sympathy.

VII. Belgium, the whole world will agree, must be evacuated and restored, without any attempt to limit the sovereignty which she enjoys in common with all other free nations. No other single act will serve as this will serve to restore confidence among the nations in the laws which they have themselves set and determined for the government of their relations with one another. Without this healing act the whole structure and validity of international law is forever impaired.

VIII. All French territory should be freed and the invaded portions restored, and the wrong done to France by Prussia in 1871 in the matter of Alsace-Lorraine, which has unsettled the peace of the world for nearly fifty years, should be righted, in order that peace may once more be made secure in the interest of all.

IX. A readjustment of the frontiers of Italy should be effected along clearly recognizable lines of nationality.

X. The peoples of Austria-Hungary, whose place among the nations we wish to see safeguarded and assured, should be accorded the freest opportunity to autonomous development.

XI. Rumania, Serbia, and Montenegro should be evacuated; occupied territories restored; Serbia accorded free and secure access to the sea; and the relations of the several Balkan states to one another determined by friendly counsel along historically established lines of allegiance and nationality; and international guarantees of the political and economic independence and territorial integrity of the several Balkan states should be entered into.

XII. The turkish portion of the present Ottoman Empire should be assured a secure sovereignty, but the other nationalities which are now under Turkish rule should be assured an undoubted security of life and an absolutely unmolested opportunity of autonomous development, and the Dardanelles should be permanently opened as a free passage to the ships and commerce of all nations under international guarantees.

XIII. An independent Polish state should be erected which should include the territories inhabited by indisputably Polish populations, which should be assured a free and secure access to the sea, and whose political and economic independence and territorial integrity should be guaranteed by international covenant.

XIV. A general association of nations must be formed under specific covenants for the purpose of affording mutual guarantees of political independence and territorial integrity to great and small states alike.

In regard to these essential rectifications of wrong and assertions of right we feel ourselves to be intimate partners of all the governments and peoples associated together against the Imperialists. We cannot be separated in interest or divided in purpose. We stand together until the end.

For such arrangements and covenants we are willing to fight and to continue to fight until they are achieved; but only because we wish the right to prevail and desire a just and stable peace such as can be secured only by removing the chief provocations to war, which this programme does remove. We have no jealousy of German greatness, and there is nothing in this programme that impairs it. We grudge her no achievement or distinction of learning or of pacific enterprise such as have made her record very bright and very enviable. We do not wish to injure her or to block in any way her legitimate influence or power. We do not wish to fight her either with arms or with hostile arrangements of trade if she is willing to associate herself with us and the other peace-loving nations of the world in covenants of justice and law and fair dealing. We wish her only to accept a place of equality among the peoples of the world,—the new world in which we now live,—instead of a place of mastery.

Not expensive passage. Got it. Can we protect Poland, too?

Yep. That's lucky number 13. And I would like to see a League of Nations to serve as a place to resolve differences between countries.

Good luck with that...

Some may call my plan idealistic. But we must stand together until the end. My goal is not to punish Germany, as we do not want to go to war ever again. But Germany must be willing to play well with others for peace to prevail. We're equals, not enemies.

That's a pretty good plan. You deserve some kind of recognition for it.

Well, don't tell anyone, but I'm going to win a Nobel Peace Prize!

THE ECONOMIC BILL OF RIGHTS

Delivered January 11, 1944

Midwestern farmer

In January 1944, Franklin Delano Roosevelt was president and World War II was coming to an end. During his State of the Union address that year, Roosevelt called for "a second Bill of Rights" to help make the lives of all Americans better and more secure. He created a list of rights that would apply to all people in our country, regardless of their race or social class. His list of rights included the right to a decent job, the right to a good home, the right to a good education, and the right to adequate medical care.

FDR delivers the State of the Union address into radio microphones on January 11, 1944.

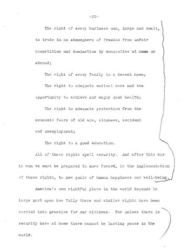

The right of every business man, large and small, to trade in an atmosphere of freedom from unfair competition and domination by monopolies at home or abroad;

The right of every family to a decent home;

The right to adequate medical care and the opportunity to achieve and enjoy good health;

The right to adequate protection from the economic fears of old age, sickness, accident and unemployment;

The right to a good education.

All of these rights spell security. And after this war is won we must be prepared to move foward, in the implementation of these rights, to new goals of human happiness and well-being.

America's own rightful place in the world depends in large part upon how fully these and similar rights have been carried into practice for our citizens. For unless there is security here at home there cannot be lasting peace in the world.

Roosevelt's draft of the speech shows notations he made before delivering it.

By using this terminology, Roosevelt was referencing the U.S. Constitution and the Bill of Rights. He believed that these social and economic rights, like the rights outlined in the original Bill of Rights, should be a defining part of our culture.

Roosevelt's Bill of Rights was never officially put into action, and his proposals did not become laws. However, his ideas influenced other presidents and inspired federal social programs that aimed to improve education and health care for all Americans.

In recent years, U.S. politicians have pushed for health-care policies that reflect the goals laid out in Roosevelt's Bill of Rights.

In 2008, presidential candidate Barack Obama used similar language to talk about health care. Obama declared that health care "should be a right for every American." To that end, after becoming president, he proposed new legislation called the Affordable Care Act, which was passed by Congress and signed into law. The role of government in health care remains a topic of debate among politicians and legislators.

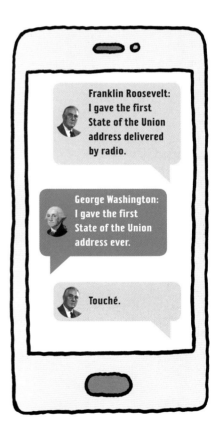

Franklin Roosevelt: I gave the first State of the Union address delivered by radio.

George Washington: I gave the first State of the Union address ever.

Touché.

It is our duty now to begin to lay the plans and determine the strategy for the winning of a lasting peace and the establishment of an American standard of living higher than ever before known. We cannot be content, no matter how high that general standard of living may be, if some fraction of our people—whether it be one-third or one-fifth or one-tenth- is ill-fed, ill-clothed, ill housed, and insecure.

This Republic had its beginning, and grew to its present strength, under the protection of certain inalienable political rights—among them the right of free speech, free press, free worship, trial by jury, freedom from unreasonable searches and seizures. They were our rights to life and liberty.

As our Nation has grown in size and stature, however— as our industrial economy expanded—these political rights proved inadequate to assure us equality in the pursuit of happiness.

We have come to a clear realization of the fact that true individual freedom cannot exist without economic security and independence. "Necessitous men are not free men." People who are hungry and out of a job are the stuff of which dictatorships are made.

In our day these economic truths have become accepted as self-evident. We have accepted, so to speak, a second Bill of Rights under which a new basis of security and prosperity can be established for all regardless of station, race, or creed.

Among these are:

> The right to a useful and remunerative job in the industries or shops or farms or mines of the Nation;
>
> The right to earn enough to provide adequate food and clothing and recreation;
>
> The right of every farmer to raise and sell his products at a return which will give him and his family a decent living;

The right of every businessman, large and small, to trade in an atmosphere of freedom from unfair competition and domination by monopolies at home or abroad;

The right of every family to a decent home;

The right to adequate medical care and the opportunity to achieve and enjoy good health;

The right to adequate protection from the economic fears of old age, sickness, accident, and unemployment;

The right to a good education.

All of these rights spell security. And after this war is won we must be prepared to move forward, in the implementation of these rights, to new goals of human happiness and well-being.

America's own rightful place in the world depends in large part upon how fully these and similar rights have been carried into practice for our citizens. For unless there is security here at home there cannot be lasting peace in the world.

I think all Americans have the right to enough food, access to medical care, and a safe place to live. I believe the government should defend those rights for our citizens. If we don't, we will lose our ability to lead in the world.

I'm in! Where do I sign?

MEET THE AUTHOR

FRANKLIN DELANO ROOSEVELT

Franklin Delano Roosevelt was the only president to be elected to four terms in office.

When he became president in 1932, the nation was suffering from the Great Depression. Roosevelt set up government agencies that created jobs, and pushed for laws that regulated fair pay. He established Social Security and insurance for the unemployed.

Roosevelt delivered his Economic Bill of Rights as part of his State of the Union address over the radio in 1944. He died in April 1945, three months into his fourth term in office.

THE TRUMAN DOCTRINE

Delivered on March 12, 1947

American schoolgirl

After World War II ended in 1945, a number of countries in Asia and Europe adopted communist governments. The Soviet Union was viewed as the center of communist activity. On March 12, 1947, President Harry S. Truman delivered a speech to Congress asking for money to help stop the spread of communism in the countries of Turkey and Greece. Truman believed that the U.S. should take an active role in world affairs, marking a shift from earlier U.S policies

Harry S. Truman delivers a speech to Congress on March 12, 1947.

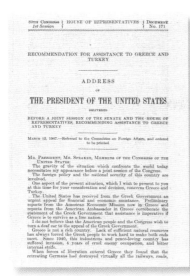

A copy of Truman's speech

that focused on isolationism and staying out of international conflicts. Truman's policies aimed at stopping communism came to be known as the Truman Doctrine, and they guided U.S. foreign policy for the next 40 years.

In February 1947, Great Britain said it could no longer provide money and military aid to assist Turkey and Greece. The U.S. feared that if these countries fell under Soviet influence, then other countries in western Europe and Africa could also fall under Soviet expansion.

Truman asserted in his speech that the world faced a choice in the years to come. He said that nations could adopt a way of life based on "the will of the majority," or they could face a way of life based on "the will of a minority forcibly imposed upon the majority." Truman said the U.S. should support free people, and not governments that relied on "terror and oppression." He argued that the U.S. needed to provide military and economic assistance to protect nations from communist aggression.

The Truman Doctrine replaced the Monroe Doctrine, which had argued for America to stay out of international affairs. Truman's policies guided U.S. and Soviet relations for the next four decades, a period called the Cold War.

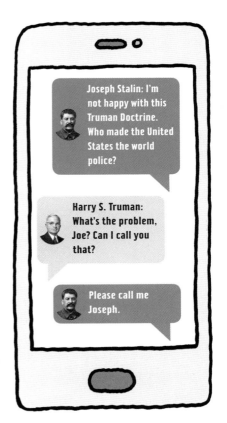

What's all this about gravity?? You guys try to blame me for everything. Even I can't control the laws of physics.

Not THAT kind of gravity. That just means this is a serious situation, Joseph.

OOOHHHH! I get it. Listen, Harry, we were pretty good partners during World War II. We really kicked some butt. What gives with the new attitude?

Sorry, Joseph. We WERE allies during the war, but only because we shared a common enemy. Now that Nazi Germany is no longer a threat, we have some serious concerns about your system of government.

Mr. President, Mr. Speaker, Members of the Congress of the United States:

The gravity of the situation which confronts the world today necessitates my appearance before a joint session of the Congress. The foreign policy and the national security of this country are involved.

One aspect of the present situation, which I wish to present to you at this time for your consideration and decision, concerns Greece and Turkey.

The United States has received from the Greek Government an urgent appeal for financial and economic assistance. Preliminary reports from the American Economic Mission now in Greece and reports from the American Ambassador in Greece corroborate the statement of the Greek Government that assistance is imperative if Greece is to survive as a free nation.

I do not believe that the American people and the Congress wish to turn a deaf ear to the appeal of the Greek Government.

Greece is not a rich country. Lack of sufficient natural resources has always forced the Greek people to work hard to make both ends meet. Since 1940, this industrious and peace loving country has suffered invasion, four years of cruel enemy occupation, and bitter internal strife.

When forces of liberation entered Greece they found that the retreating Germans had destroyed virtually all the railways, roads, port facilities, communications, and merchant marine. More than a thousand villages had been burned. Eighty-five per cent of the children were tubercular. Livestock, poultry, and draft animals had almost disappeared. Inflation had wiped out practically all savings.

As a result of these tragic conditions, a militant minority, exploiting human want and misery, was able to create political chaos which, until now, has made economic recovery impossible.

Greece is today without funds to finance the importation of those goods which are essential to bare subsistence. Under these circumstances the people of Greece cannot make progress in solving their problems of reconstruction. Greece is in desperate need of financial and economic assistance to enable it to resume purchases of food, clothing, fuel and seeds. These are indispensable for the subsistence of its people and are obtainable only from abroad. Greece must have help to import the goods necessary to restore internal order and security, so essential for economic and political recovery.

The Greek Government has also asked for the assistance of experienced American administrators, economists and technicians to insure that the financial and other aid given to Greece shall be used effectively in creating a stable and self-sustaining economy and in improving its public administration.

The very existence of the Greek state is today threatened by the terrorist activities of several thousand armed men, led by Communists, who defy the government's authority at a number of points, particularly along the northern boundaries. A Commission appointed by the United Nations security Council is at present investigating disturbed conditions in northern Greece and alleged border violations along the frontier between Greece on the one hand and Albania, Bulgaria, and Yugoslavia on the other.

Meanwhile, the Greek Government is unable to cope with the situation. The Greek army is small and poorly equipped. It needs supplies and equipment if it is to restore the authority of the government throughout Greek territory. Greece must have assistance if it is to become a self-supporting and self-respecting democracy.

The United States must supply that assistance. We have already extended to Greece certain types of relief and economic aid but these are inadequate.

I believe it's in the best interest of the American people to promote democracy throughout the world.

Hannah Schoolgirl: I have a thing or two to say about that. After all, I'm an American.

Okay, Hannah—shoot.

I don't know so much about what's going on in Greece and Turkey, but I do know that wars cost a lot of money. Maybe picking a fight with the Soviet Union isn't such a good idea.

We're not exactly picking a fight with the Soviet Union. That's not how a cold war works. Instead of confronting the bad guys directly, we'll just aid the people fighting against them throughout the world.

Hey, Dean. Stalin's been blowin' up my phone. He's worried that the Truman Doctrine will prevent him from spreading the influence of the Soviet Union around the world.

Dean Acheson: That's kind of the point, Harry. Greece has been in bad shape since the Germans invaded. Now that WWII is over, the Soviet Union is the greatest threat to world peace.

I know. You've said that before.

We cannot allow dictatorships where a few leaders loyal to the Soviet Union impose their will and ideas upon whole countries. We must help Greece become a democracy!

I know, I know. Great Britain has stopped sending aid now that the war is over. So we need to help a country out. And let's help Turkey, too.

Noooooooooooooooo, not Turkey!

There is no other country to which democratic Greece can turn.

No other nation is willing and able to provide the necessary support for a democratic Greek government.

The British Government, which has been helping Greece, can give no further financial or economic aid after March 31. Great Britain finds itself under the necessity of reducing or liquidating its commitments in several parts of the world, including Greece.

We have considered how the United Nations might assist in this crisis. But the situation is an urgent one requiring immediate action and the United Nations and its related organizations are not in a position to extend help of the kind that is required.

It is important to note that the Greek Government has asked for our aid in utilizing effectively the financial and other assistance we may give to Greece, and in improving its public administration. It is of the utmost importance that we supervise the use of any funds made available to Greece; in such a manner that each dollar spent will count toward making Greece self-supporting, and will help to build an economy in which a healthy democracy can flourish.

No government is perfect. One of the chief virtues of a democracy, however, is that its defects are always visible and under democratic processes can be pointed out and corrected. The Government of Greece is not perfect. Nevertheless it represents eighty-five per cent of the members of the Greek Parliament who were chosen in an election last year. Foreign observers, including 692 Americans, considered this election to be a fair expression of the views of the Greek people.

The Greek Government has been operating in an atmosphere of chaos and extremism. It has made mistakes. The extension of aid by this country does not mean that the United States condones everything that the Greek Government has done or will do. We have condemned in the past, and we condemn now, extremist measures of the right or the left. We have in the past advised tolerance, and we advise tolerance now.

Greece's neighbor, Turkey, also deserves our attention.

The future of Turkey as an independent and economically sound state is clearly no less important to the freedom-loving peoples of the world than the future of Greece. The circumstances in which Turkey finds itself today are considerably different from those of Greece. Turkey has been spared the disasters that have beset Greece. And during the war, the United States and Great Britain furnished Turkey with material aid.

Nevertheless, Turkey now needs our support.

Since the war Turkey has sought financial assistance from Great Britain and the United States for the purpose of effecting that modernization necessary for the maintenance of its national integrity.

That integrity is essential to the preservation of order in the Middle East.

The British government has informed us that, owing to its own difficulties can no longer extend financial or economic aid to Turkey.

As in the case of Greece, if Turkey is to have the assistance it needs, the United States must supply it. We are the only country able to provide that help.

I am fully aware of the broad implications involved if the United States extends assistance to Greece and Turkey, and I shall discuss these implications with you at this time.

One of the primary objectives of the foreign policy of the United States is the creation of conditions in which we and other nations will be able to work out a way of life free from coercion. This was a fundamental issue in the war with Germany and Japan. Our victory

Turkey is just as important as Greece, even if it hasn't had the setbacks that Greece had to deal with.

But we need the Dardanelles and Turkish Straits. That would give us control of the waterway from the Black Sea to the Mediterranean.

Not gonna happen, Joseph. If the British won't take care of it, it's our responsibility to help. At least until I can get the United Nations under way.

Sheesh. It's not like we haven't done this before. The U.S. has been defending North and South America since the Monroe Doctrine. This is an expansion of that policy.

But this is our neighborhood! What's your beef with the Soviet Union?

If Greece falls under communist control, then who's to say Turkey isn't next? Confusion and disorder will run rampant throughout the entire Middle East and maybe even the world! We need to support free people, with open governments, free press and radio (AKA free speech—we have an amendment for that), and open elections.

Good call, Harry, but it could use a better name. In the 1950s, President Dwight D. Eisenhower is going to call it the Domino Theory. Same idea, but it's definitely catchier.

was won over countries which sought to impose their will, and their way of life, upon other nations.

To ensure the peaceful development of nations, free from coercion, the United States has taken a leading part in establishing the United Nations, The United Nations is designed to make possible lasting freedom and independence for all its members. We shall not realize our objectives, however, unless we are willing to help free peoples to maintain their free institutions and their national integrity against aggressive movements that seek to impose upon them totalitarian regimes. This is no more than a frank recognition that totalitarian regimes imposed on free peoples, by direct or indirect aggression, undermine the foundations of international peace and hence the security of the United States.

The peoples of a number of countries of the world have recently had totalitarian regimes forced upon them against their will. The Government of the United States has made frequent protests against coercion and intimidation, in violation of the Yalta agreement, in Poland, Rumania, and Bulgaria. I must also state

MEET THE AUTHOR

HARRY S. TRUMAN

Harry S. Truman joined President Franklin Delano Roosevelt's presidential ticket in 1944, and was elected vice president. He had been vice president for only 82 days when President Roosevelt died. Suddenly, Truman was president.

World War II wasn't over yet. Truman ordered the use of the atomic bomb against Japan. The Japanese surrendered. After the war, Truman was concerned about the spread of communism. The Truman Doctrine reflected his belief that the United States should stop the spread of communism elsewhere in the world. In 1950, Truman followed the doctrine when he sent troops to South Korea to help defend it against communist-backed North Korea.

that in a number of other countries there have been similar developments.

At the present moment in world history nearly every nation must choose between alternative ways of life. The choice is too often not a free one.

One way of life is based upon the will of the majority, and is distinguished by free institutions, representative government, free elections, guarantees of individual liberty, freedom of speech and religion, and freedom from political oppression.

The second way of life is based upon the will of a minority forcibly imposed upon the majority. It relies upon terror and oppression, a controlled press and radio; fixed elections, and the suppression of personal freedoms.

I believe that it must be the policy of the United States to support free peoples who are resisting attempted subjugation by armed minorities or by outside pressures.

I believe that we must assist free peoples to work out their own destinies in their own way.

I believe that our help should be primarily through economic and financial aid which is essential to economic stability and orderly political processes.

The world is not static, and the status quo is not sacred. But we cannot allow changes in the status quo in violation of the Charter of the United Nations by such methods as coercion, or by such subterfuges as political infiltration. In helping free and independent nations to maintain their freedom, the United States will be giving effect to the principles of the Charter of the United Nations.

It is necessary only to glance at a map to realize that the survival and integrity of the Greek nation are of grave importance in a much wider situation. If Greece should fall under the control of an armed minority, the effect upon its neighbor, Turkey, would

Hi. Hannah again! I like the idea of assisting free people in the world. But how is this going to work in the future? Are we going to become the global sheriff? Will we police the whole world, aiming to spread democracy and peace?

That's a fair point. I guess the answer is yes...

Listen to the little girl, Harry. Why can't we all just go our separate ways?

I don't think the world has to stay exactly the same, but I do think that we have to guard against changes brought by subterfuge or political coercion.

What does THAT mean?

People throughout the world should be able to choose their governments, free from misinformation, vote rigging, or threats.

be immediate and serious. Confusion and disorder might well spread throughout the entire Middle East.

Moreover, the disappearance of Greece as an independent state would have a profound effect upon those countries in Europe whose peoples are struggling against great difficulties to maintain their freedoms and their independence while they repair the damages of war.

It would be an unspeakable tragedy if these countries, which have struggled so long against overwhelming odds, should lose that victory for which they sacrificed so much. Collapse of free institutions and loss of independence would be disastrous not only for them but for the world. Discouragement and possibly failure would quickly be the lot of neighboring peoples striving to maintain their freedom and independence.

Should we fail to aid Greece and Turkey in this fateful hour, the effect will be far reaching to the West as well as to the East.

We must take immediate and resolute action.

I therefore ask the Congress to provide authority for assistance to Greece and Turkey in the amount of $400,000,000 for the period ending June 30, 1948. In requesting these funds, I have taken into consideration the maximum amount of relief assistance which would be furnished to Greece out of the $350,000,000 which I recently requested that the Congress authorize for the prevention of starvation and suffering in countries devastated by the war.

In addition to funds, I ask the Congress to authorize the detail of American civilian and military personnel to Greece and Turkey, at the request of those countries, to assist in the tasks of reconstruction, and for the purpose of supervising the use of such financial and material assistance as may be furnished. I recommend that authority also be provided for the instruction and training of selected Greek and Turkish personnel.

Holy moly! Did you say 400 million dollars down there?

I did. But I also said that it would be a tragedy if these countries that fought so hard for their independence lost it now through our inaction.

I get that, but this is 1948. 400 million dollars is a lot of money! I could buy a ton of bubble gum with that.

That girl is smart. I'm with Hannah!

I fear the consequences of not helping our allies would be far worse.

Finally, I ask that the Congress provide authority which will permit the speediest and most effective use, in terms of needed commodities, supplies, and equipment, of such funds as may be authorized.

If further funds, or further authority, should be needed for purposes indicated in this message, I shall not hesitate to bring the situation before the Congress. On this subject the Executive and Legislative branches of the Government must work together.

This is a serious course upon which we embark.

I would not recommend it except that the alternative is much more serious. The United States contributed $341,000,000,000 toward winning World War II. This is an investment in world freedom and world peace.

The assistance that I am recommending for Greece and Turkey amounts to little more than 1 tenth of 1 per cent of this investment. It is only common sense that we should safeguard this investment and make sure that it was not in vain.

The seeds of totalitarian regimes are nurtured by misery and want. They spread and grow in the evil soil of poverty and strife. They reach their full growth when the hope of a people for a better life has died. We must keep that hope alive.

The free peoples of the world look to us for support in maintaining their freedoms.

If we falter in our leadership, we may endanger the peace of the world—and we shall surely endanger the welfare of our own nation.

Great responsibilities have been placed upon us by the swift movement of events.

I am confident that the Congress will face these responsibilities squarely.

You do make some good points. I'll reserve judgment for a couple of years. We'll see how this whole Cold War pans out.

Well, this is going to work out pretty well. In a couple of months, the funds for Greece will be approved. Your doctrine will be the start of a long campaign against the spread of communism, known as the Cold War.

BRRRRRRRRRRRRRR. It's getting cold in here!

BUILDING BLOCKS FOR A DEMOCRACY

Documents large and small have shaped American history, for better and for worse. Studying them is a great way to learn more about the course our history has taken. Here are some of the important laws, letters, and speeches that have led us to where we are today.

1620 The **Mayflower Compact** established governing rules for the Plymouth Colony, one of the earliest settlements in North America. Signed by 41 men aboard the *Mayflower*, the Compact is a short document that binds its signers to agreeing to work together as a single government. Although it is a fairly short and vague document, it introduced an important idea for American government: that people can establish a government for themselves by mutual consent of the governed.

1776 ## The Declaration of Independence

1777 Shortly before the end of the Revolutionary War, the 13 fledgling states agreed on a framework for their association. The **Articles of Confederation** (ratified 1781) was a loosely binding charter that declared a nation without truly creating one. The Articles created a government run by a Congress in which each state had an equal vote and where important measures required the consent of at least nine states. Congress had no power to regulate trade, to impose taxes without the unanimous agreement of all the states, or even to compel states to carry out its directives. While the Articles were a failure and quickly replaced, they were an important stepping-stone toward the Constitution.

1787 ## The U.S. Constitution (ratified 1788)

1787-88 Once the Constitution was drafted, it still needed to be ratified, or approved, by nine states before it could take effect. Three of the Framers—Alexander Hamilton, John Jay, and James Madison—wrote 85 essays arguing for ratification. All were published under the same pen name: Publius. The **Federalist Papers**, as they came to be known, provide unique insight into the Framers' intentions in drafting the Constitution.

1796

Toward the end of his second term, President George Washington began drafting a goodbye to the American people. **Washington's Farewell Address** was revised considerably by Alexander Hamilton and completed in 1796. Among other things, Washington warned the American public of the dangers of slipping into partisan politics, of developing a large and entrenched military, and of entering into permanent alliances with foreign countries.

1803

Signed by the United States and France on April 30, 1803, the **Louisiana Purchase** paved the way for the nation's westward expansion. Under the terms of the deal, the U.S. spent about $15 million for 828,000 square miles west of the Mississippi River. This territory would later become part or all of 15 states, including Louisiana, Missouri, Oklahoma, Kansas, North Dakota, New Mexico, Minnesota, Wyoming, and Colorado. The Louisiana Purchase territory soon became central to the question of slavery, and whether slavery would be permitted in the new states that were formed in this area.

1823

The Monroe Doctrine

1830

The **Indian Removal Act** marked the beginning of a period of intense persecution of American Indians in the United States. Signed by President Andrew Jackson on May 28, 1830, the act gave the president authority to negotiate treaties with Indian nations in order to move them from their lands. Hundreds of thousands of American Indians were forced to leave their homes because of the act. Cherokee Indians in Georgia, North Carolina, Tennessee, and Alabama were removed as a result of the Treaty of New Echota, signed under the Indian Removal Act in 1835. Although many Cherokee had opposed the treaty, they were nevertheless required to abide by it once it was signed. In 1838 and 1839, 16,000 Cherokee Indians were forced to relocate to "Indian Territory," walking along what has come to be called the Trail of Tears. Approximately 4,000 died along the way.

1862

President Abraham Lincoln signed the **Homestead Act** on May 20, 1862. It offered up 160 acres of public land to anyone who was willing to occupy it for at least five years. The Homestead Act spurred a rush of westward migration. More than 80,000 acres of public land were given away over the next 18 years.

1863 The Emancipation Proclamation

1863 On November 19, 1863, President Abraham Lincoln gave a speech to dedicate a new cemetery in Gettysburg, Pennsylvania. Just 272 words long, it became one of the most beloved speeches in American history. Delivered in the middle of the Civil War, the **Gettysburg Address** captured the reasons for fighting the war. Lincoln promised the nation that "government of the people, by the people, and for the people, shall not perish from the earth."

1887 Named for Senator Henry Laurens Dawes and signed by President Grover Cleveland on February 8, 1887, the **Dawes Act** was an attempt to strip American Indians of their "Indianness" and force them to assimilate into American culture. The act broke apart reservations and allotted the land to individual members of a tribe, rather than the tribe as a whole. It also forced the tribes to give up their tribal governments and resulted in much of the Indian land being sold to white settlers. Lawmakers hoped that breaking up the tribes and giving individuals their own land to farm would loosen bonds within the tribes and that, as farmers, American Indians would give up Indian culture in favor of American. The act was amended several times.

1890 Named for Senator John Sherman and signed by President Benjamin Harrison on July 2, 1890, the **Sherman Antitrust Act** was passed by a nearly unanimous vote—with only one vote against it. The law gave the federal government the authority to prevent businesses from forming trusts, arrangements in which stockholders of multiple companies in the same industry would pool their shares in exchange for a share of profits from the group. The trusts eliminated competition and led to unfair labor practices and pricing. The Sherman Antitrust Act and the Clayton Antitrust Act form the basis for the government's efforts in preventing monopolies, an important part of maintaining a free and open market.

1896

In 1892, a black train passenger named Homer Plessy refused to sit in a black-designated train car in Louisiana. He was arrested and charged with violating a Louisiana law that required blacks and whites to sit in separate train cars. He contended that the law was a violation of his constitutional rights under the 13th and 14th Amendments of the Constitution. The Supreme Court considered the case in *Plessy v. Ferguson* in 1896. In a 7–1 decision, the justices held that the law was allowable because it offered "separate but equal" accommodations for different races. The *Plessy v. Ferguson* decision served as the legal defense for segregation laws for nearly 60 years before it was finally overturned in 1954.

1918

The 14 Points

1935

On August 14, 1935, President Franklin Delano Roosevelt signed the **Social Security Act**. It created the government's first national program to provide financial support for workers. Social Security was launched during the Great Depression, when many people lost their financial security and their life savings. The program lent a helping hand to those in need. In 1939, benefits for family members were added.

1942

On February 19, 1942, a little more than two months after the Japanese attack on Pearl Harbor, President Franklin Delano Roosevelt signed **Executive Order 9066**. It required first-generation Japanese Americans to leave their homes and move to internment camps. In all, about 122,000 people (nearly 70,000 of whom were American citizens) were forced to sell their homes and businesses and move to the camps, which were located in remote areas of Wyoming, California, Utah, Arizona, Colorado, Idaho, and Arkansas. The order was a clear violation of the internees' constitutional rights, causing them to be held without charge, and placed an immense burden on them. Today, many consider Executive Order 9066—a harsh and illegal order created by an otherwise popular president—an example of the dangers posed by laws based on xenophobia and fear.

1944

The Economic Bill of Rights

The Truman Doctrine

Created by George C. Marshall, who was secretary of state under President Harry S. Truman, the **Marshall Plan** was a strategy for providing economic support to help western European countries rebuild after World War II. Following World War I, harsh economic conditions led directly to the rise of Nazism in Germany and the start of the Second World War. Truman recognized the need to stabilize the economies of western European countries and to help them recover from the devastation of the war. Over the next four years, the Economic Cooperation Administration, which had been formed under the plan, loaned $13 billion to 16 countries. The plan is credited with providing a lasting foundation for peace in the region.

1954

Following the Supreme Court's decision in *Plessy v. Ferguson* in 1896, Southern states had been free to pass laws segregating their citizens by race. In 1954, several court cases challenging the legality of school segregation were considered by the Supreme Court. On May 17, 1954, the Supreme Court ruled for Linda Brown in a case called ***Brown v. Board of Education of Topeka***. Linda was a black girl who had been disallowed from attending a white school near her home in Topeka, Kansas. The court ruled that school segregation was a violation of the 14th Amendment of the Constitution and that separate was inherently unequal. The ruling was a huge step in the fight for equal rights and provided the basis for overturning Jim Crow laws throughout the South.

1963

On August 28, 1963, more than 250,000 people gathered at the Lincoln Memorial in Washington, D.C., to demand equality and jobs for all Americans. Reverend Martin Luther King, Jr., delivered a speech that would be quoted over and over for decades to come. His **"I Have a Dream"** speech was a powerful statement about the need for racial equality in the U.S. "I have a dream," he said, "that one day this nation will rise up, live out the true meaning of its creed: 'We hold these truths to be self-evident, that all men are created equal.' . . . I have a dream that my four little children will one day live in a nation where they will not be judged by the color of their skin but by the content of their character."

1963 In the years following the development of the atomic bomb, the United States and Soviet Union rushed to develop more effective nuclear weapons. As part of the arms race, both nations conducted nuclear tests on land, on Pacific islands, and in the atmosphere. By the 1950s, it became clear that aboveground nuclear weapons testing was spreading radioactive fallout around the world. The U.S., the Soviet Union, Great Britain, Canada, and France negotiated for eight years before completing the **Limited Nuclear Test Ban Treaty**, which was finally signed on August 5, 1963. It prohibited the testing of nuclear arms in the water, the atmosphere, and outer space.

1964 Signed by President Lyndon B. Johnson on July 2, 1964, the **Civil Rights Act** made it illegal to discriminate against anyone on the basis of their race in public places, employment, housing, and education.

1965 Signed by President Lyndon B. Johnson on August 6, 1965, the **Voting Rights Act** outlawed various practices that were designed to stop black citizens from voting, including literacy tests and poll taxes. It also established the role of federal examiners to monitor elections and ensure that the law was being followed.

1972

On June 23, 1972, President Richard M. Nixon signed **Title IX**, a federal law that prohibits discrimination based on gender in schools that receive government funds. Before Title IX, many colleges limited the number of women who could attend, and few offered women athletic scholarships. In high schools, girls were discouraged from studying subjects such as math and science. Title IX was intended to ensure that girls have the same opportunities as boys, in the classroom and on the playing field. Today, supporters point to Title IX's successes. In 1971, only 18 percent of U.S. women completed college. Now there are more women than men in U.S. colleges. Fewer than 30,000 women participated in college sports in 1972. By 2003, some 160,000 college women were competing.

1973 In a 7–2 decision that came down on January 22, 1973, the Supreme Court ruled in a case called *Roe v. Wade* that laws restricting women's reproductive rights violate the right to privacy under the Constitution. The case has been central to debate surrounding women's rights for decades.

1987

Following World War II, Germany was divided in two. West Germany was a democratic country while East Germany was communist. The capital city of Berlin, located in East Germany, was similarly divided. Democratic West Berlin was entirely surrounded by a wall that cut it off from the communist areas that surrounded it. On June 12, 1987, U.S. president Ronald Reagan delivered a rousing **speech at the Brandenburg Gate**. He called on the Soviet premier, Mikhail Gorbachev, to tear down the Berlin Wall. The speech inspired many and helped fuel the push in the Soviet Union to open borders. The Berlin Wall finally came down on November 9, 1989.

2010

Signed by President Barack Obama on March 23, 2010, the **Affordable Care Act** aimed to provide American citizens with better health insurance by expanding coverage, lowering costs, and guaranteeing more choices in health-care providers. The law was far from perfect. Many were frustrated by the requirement that all citizens have health insurance or pay a penalty, and its rollout was plagued with technical problems. But the law helped bring coverage to millions of Americans who had previously been unable to get it as a result of low income or pre-existing medical conditions. The law also underlined the frustration Americans felt over the state of the health-care system and highlighted their desire for better health care for all. The Affordable Care Act had an enormous effect on American politics and continues to be a subject of debate and reform efforts today.

INDEX